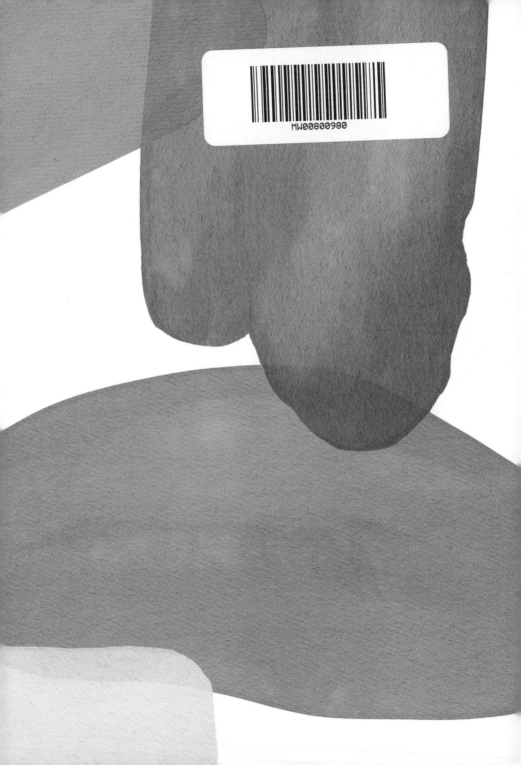

A MILLION TINY MOMENTS

EMILY A. JENSEN & LAURA WIFLER

HARVEST HOUSE PUBLISHERS
EUGENE, OREGON

Published in association with the literary agency of Wolgemuth & Wilson

Cover design by Connie Gabbert Design + Illustration
Cover & interior images © West Wind Creative / Creative Market
Art direction by Nicole Dougherty
Interior design by Janelle Coury

For bulk, special sales, or ministry purchases, please call 1-800-547-8979.
Email: CustomerService@hhbooks.com

This logo is a federally registered trademark of the Hawkins Children's LLC. Harvest House Publishers, Inc., is the exclusive licensee of this trademark.

A MILLION TINY MOMENTS

Copyright © 2025 by Emily A. Jensen and Laura Wifler
Published by Harvest House Publishers
Eugene, Oregon 97408
www.harvesthousepublishers.com

ISBN 978-0-7369-8854-4 (hardcover)
ISBN 978-0-7369-8855-1 (eBook)
ISBN 978-0-7369-9210-7 (eAudio)

Library of Congress Control Number: 2024942253

Printed in China

24 25 26 27 28 29 30 31 32 / RDS / 10 9 8 7 6 5 4 3 2 1

CONTENTS

INTRODUCTION

Motherhood is lived in a million tiny moments. A moment with hot coffee in our favorite chair before rising to tend to a newborn's cry. A moment to admire the laughter among siblings. A moment to sneak a square of chocolate in the pantry or to laugh at an eight-year-old's joke. Like an old-fashioned photo reel, the moments flash by in our minds: holding her against your skin for the first time, sharing the same slide at the park, rocking him in that old chair, seeing her blow out five candles on the cake. The highlights hit us like little light beams, and the moments meld together to become the spectacularly bright thing we know as motherhood.

But not every moment is one we want to remember. Not every moment is good or joyful, silly or fun, nostalgic or mundane. Some of them are just plain hard. Or sad. Or painful. A moment of sobbing after a trip to the doctor. A moment of yelling after losing our cool from all the running and the noise. A moment of panic after an unexpected phone call. A moment of rumination and shame while we lie in bed and recount the day. All of us find moments of darkness speckled in among the light beams of motherhood, and we're not always sure what to do with them.

Over a decade into motherhood, we (Emily and Laura) have lived our own montage of moments, and we understand how precious, varied, and complex they are. How some of them feel as if they are going to drag on forever (we're looking at you, "little years") and some of them feel as if they are flying by too fast. (Is ten the perfect childhood age? Seems pretty close!) And something we've learned is that every one of those moments—good, bad, or in between—matters.

We don't say this to give you a guilt trip or one more thing you need to worry about trying to maximize, capture, or enjoy. (Moms have plenty of that!) No, it's not as if *every single second* is high-stakes and you have to get it right—or else. But every moment matters because you matter. And your children matter. And all the people who you come in contact with—for that matter—matter! The moments of your motherhood are important because God knew every one of them before you were born (Psalm 139:16). They matter because you have a sacred mission and purpose to love God, worship and serve him above all else, and love others (Matthew 28:19-20; Isaiah 43:7). They matter because if you love God and follow him, your steps are established by God (Proverbs 16:9). He looks over all the earth, and nothing escapes his notice or control (Job 28:24). They matter because God says they matter (Ecclesiastes 12:13-14).

Feel a little heady and overwhelming? It takes time to understand our lives through this lens, but it's not impossible. It takes growth and practice. But if *we* can do it, *you* can do it too. Over the years, our heart and mission for moms have never changed. This book has one primary goal: to point moms to look beyond their moments to the One who holds all your moments.

We want you to know that you were created good, as God's image-bearer.

But because of the Fall, things in life and motherhood (and especially in our own hearts) won't always be good, understandable, or honor God. But there's good news for all of us—when we recognize our own inabilities and insufficiencies and put our faith in Jesus Christ, trusting him as our Lord and Savior, we have new life, new hope, and new purpose. This, all of this, is the gospel. Through it, our moments take on a whole different meaning, and that changes everything. Because in Christ, we're not just living for peace and quiet, surviving until becoming empty-nesters, or looking back at nostalgic memories, our kids' special awards, or epic family vacations (though all of those things are probably awesome). We're living for Christ himself.

Mom, the million tiny moments that make up your motherhood are given to you by God for his glory and your ultimate good (Romans 8:28; Ephesians 1:4-6). There is no moment outside of his sovereign control. No moment too small to matter. No moment too difficult or shameful. The gospel matters for each and every one of them. God wants you to turn from your sin and trust in Christ for eternal life. And when you do that, the meaning behind the million tiny moments of motherhood changes. Now they aren't just lived for the momentary happiness they can provide—they are lived for Jesus. You live a risen motherhood.

What you'll find in these pages is the narrative of two imperfect moms working out how to live for Jesus in every moment of motherhood. And we hope that it inspires and encourages you to do the same.

HOW TO READ THIS BOOK

In the following pages, you'll read a curated, edited, and updated collection of writings we've done over the years on the topic of motherhood. These entries were written during our time at Risen Motherhood, a ministry we cofounded to help moms understand what it means to live for God and follow him. Over the years at that ministry, we spoke and wrote countless words. Some of these were published on social media, some on our website, some in emails or as part of a download. We believe many of these writings hold treasures for moms beyond the life of the ministry. Had we not compiled these into a book, they would have been buried on the internet forever.

When we wrote most of these, we were moms of young children ourselves. We were wading through the little years and learning to turn our eyes to Christ in all things. Because these writings are from our hearts, they flow from our own personal experiences. This is why you'll find that topically, they aren't comprehensive. We wrote more frequently about topics that we were personally passionate about or that intersected our lives. For that reason, as an example, you'll find a few selections on disability and none on miscarriage, because both of us have a child with a disability, but neither of us have had a miscarriage.

We know we have not covered all the ways that moms can and do need practical help. Please know that even as we encourage moms to hope in Jesus and believe the truth, we don't want to brush over the many other tangible and immediate ways moms need help. If you find yourself reading these writings while you face a complex or painful situation, know that you can and should engage people in your real life and potentially seek professional help and guidance. You'll find a lot of feelings and reflections in these pieces, and in some cases, they intentionally leave you hanging so you can consider what these truths mean for your own life. Take what's helpful from each entry and leave the rest.

Finally, most of these writings are short, reflective, and feel more poetic. They don't have thesis statements and topic sentences. We chose to organize them loosely by theme, so you can read them one after the other (like a traditional book), or you can choose to search for a specific topic and reference what you need that day.

However you engage with this book, we pray it serves you.

FOR WHEN
YOU ARE TIRED

———————

Mom, you can trust in the sovereignty of God.
He feeds the sparrow, causes the oak to
grow, and raises the white lilies from their
beds each spring. He knows your needs
and will meet you where you are.

LAURA

WHEN YOU
ARE WORN OUT

LAURA

Moms want to see results. We want to see something from our efforts and know we're making a difference. We want to know we're heroes in someone's story. But when all we're doing most of the day is picking up fuzz, crumbs, and toys off the floor, it can be hard to see. Our work feels very…small.

The truth is, motherhood is not small work. Yes, it is a slow process, and it's one that isn't obvious or grand to the world. But while it's hard to see in the middle of wiping counters, scrubbing stains, and picking up sidewalk chalk, our investment as mothers will yield results of eternal value. We want instant gratification—to see our lives used in one big, heroic way—but instead, God asks for our heroism to come in the form of thousands of blurred-together days: making lunches, putting on Band-Aids, and giving kisses at bedtime tuck-ins.

Moms, our labor of finding the lost shoe and reuniting it with its match is not wasted time. That shoe is valuable work—missional work. Motherhood is about being faithful in the mundane things because we understand the bigger story we're caught up in—how we were once lost to sin and death, but we have been found and healed by the true hero, Jesus Christ. We are now instruments of God's grace, sacrifice, and perseverance, and each day, we have the privilege of reflecting him to our children.

So today, when you are feeling frazzled, alone, worn out, or just plain fed up, remember why we do this: You are not just changing diapers, scrubbing the toilet, or picking the towels up off the floor for the five hundredth time—in a million tiny moments, you are looking to the Lord and raising hearts. It's not small work. It's grand, majestic, heroic work because you're doing it in and through Christ for an eternal purpose that lasts far beyond this life.

WHEN MOTHERHOOD ISN'T WHAT YOU EXPECTED

EMILY

Have you ever imagined an ideal day of motherhood? In my imagination, the kids sleep quietly late into the morning. I have uninterrupted quiet time and at least one cup of coffee before greeting anyone. Breakfast is bountiful and received with thanksgiving. People take turns talking, and not a drop of milk falls out of place. I check everything off my list, plus I have extra time to read a book. Questions are framed politely. Everyone gets what they need by themselves. There are no surprises, and no one runs late or needs discipline. I'm in a great mood and don't struggle with impatience or discontentment. Summed up in a sentence? Everything goes right.

While each mom's ideal day looks different, most of us imagine that joy lies just on the other side of that perfect day. We think that if people were just where they were supposed to be, doing what they were supposed to be doing, we'd finally grasp joy. We determine that if we got ourselves together and did a better job of home management, meal planning, and schedule finessing, we'd find balance and experience deep happiness. Or maybe motherhood is already so far from our ideal picture because of unexpected medical challenges, long seasons of infertility or multiple miscarriages, extended-family estrangement, or marital strain—we're convinced joy is out of reach.

But if circumstances are the obstacle between us and joy, how can we grasp it? I don't know about you, but I've never had a day like the ideal one I described. Motherhood itself is a gift, and there have been many beautiful moments, but it's never long before hard things come.

Facing a less-than-ideal version of motherhood leads me down several paths, but usually not the path of joy. I'm tempted to lose hope and get cynical or crabby. I start to focus more on what I don't have instead of enjoying what I do. Maybe you don't struggle with those things, but a less-than-ideal day causes you to go into "fix-it" mode—making more lists, taking on more projects, or correcting everything that doesn't meet your standards.

I doubt any of us are on track to have our ideal day of motherhood. Even as you read this, you might be so far behind on your lists, so deep into relational conflicts or wrong reactions that you think it's impossible to recover—that all hope for joy is lost. But remember, because joy isn't found in your circumstances, it's not too far gone! Turn away from staring down your day and look to Christ himself. Let your heart swell with gratitude for how good, merciful, gracious, and steadfast he is. Think about him sitting at the right hand of God, praying for you, and have joy. Motherhood isn't perfect, but he is.

WHEN YOU FEEL LIKE A WEAK MOM

EMILY

When my first son was a toddler, I remember seeing a book with a mom laid flat on her back on the front cover. She looked exhausted and overwhelmed...*weak*. I remember scrolling by it, thinking, "I hope I never need a book like that!"

Well, fast-forward to being a mom of five (ages five and under), and somewhere in there, *it happened*. I'm not sure of the exact day, but I transformed from a "strong" mom into a "weak" mom. I started losing my patience, my energy ran low, and I saw my inability to be enough for everyone. If you were to take a picture of my heart, it looked more like the mom on the cover of that book.

There's no question—I had a lot to learn about what it meant to care for myself well and receive the help of others in motherhood. There were many areas where I was trying to go it alone and I had unrealistic expectations for myself. But at the heart of this, I was also dealing with a question of identity.

When I thought of myself primarily as a "strong" mom, I tended to be prideful, judgmental, and convinced I had the stuff good moms were made of. But when I thought of myself primarily as a "weak" mom, I felt hopeless and buried under heaps of self-pity and condemnation.

But then I remembered—I am a mom with weaknesses and limitations, but my identity is that of a "redeemed" mom.

In Christ, it's okay to be needy, but there is nothing left for me to earn, prove, or posture for. God sought me at my worst and put his Spirit in me so I could walk in his ways and share his love with others. And because of the wonderful freedom he purchased for me, I am able to rest in his strength and goodness.

Moms, wherever you are today—feeling strong or weak or somewhere in between—remember that if you are a follower of Christ, there is one story that defines you and one person who tells you who you truly are.

WHEN YOU HAVE
A HARD DAY

LAURA

If today has been a hard day, remember, it doesn't change the truth of God's grace for you. Your purpose, your goal, your mission, is still the same. His grace is sufficient.

You love God—more than anything. You say that on the good days; now you must believe that on the hard days. His grace is sufficient.

So stand straight on your wobbly legs, and trust him as you go about your day. His grace is sufficient.

Tomorrow is a new day, and with it, light will come. Remember and believe: His grace is sufficient.

WHEN GOD DOESN'T FEEL PRESENT

LAURA

Sometimes, in the chaos of children and cooking and cleaning and errands and just generally managing a household and family, I forget why I'm doing what I'm doing. I forget who I serve. I get so focused on the here and now, I forget God and eternity. Last night, as I was cooking dinner, my husband was working late, and the kids were whining at my feet, I felt exasperated. Strung out. Overwhelmed.

And then, in the middle of it all, I stopped and sang a worship song to the Lord. Asking him to remind me of his presence.

Our homes are holy. They are places set apart for God and his work. God is not afraid of your crumb-filled kitchen floors or dirt-streaked walls. You don't have to be sitting in a church pew with a steeple overhead to worship him.

God meets you exactly where you're at. He is the God of thrown-together dinners, traffic in the carpool lane, and Magna-Tiles strewn on the living room floor. He is the God of water tables and playgrounds, drives home from work, and doctor's appointments. God is everywhere! He is in everything! He needs nothing!

Remember that God's presence is in your home, Mom. Remember him at your family dinners, your playdates, your bedtimes, and in the middle of toddler tantrums. In the midst of the chaos in your house, slow down and see his glory. Be overcome by his presence. You have been equipped for this by the power of the Holy Spirit. God is the reason why we do what we do.

Stay focused on what matters.

WHEN THE JOB FEELS SMALL

LAURA

You carry a lot of things, Mom. You carry the diapers, you carry the wipes, you carry the 55 bowls that your kid just handed you. None of those jobs are too small, too meaningless, too mundane, or too beneath you when they're done in service to the glory of God.

FOR THE CARE OF INFANTS

EMILY

Nursery workers, grandmas, foster parents, caregivers, and (of course) mamas—listen up!

It might seem like what you're doing isn't *that* big of a deal. It might feel like *anyone* can change diapers or give bottles or rock a baby. And yes, to some extent, that's true. But you are doing so much more than *just* meeting physical needs.

When you choose to love an infant well—singing that quiet song, using that dorky voice, smiling in that silly way, reading that repetitive book, or feeding that messy snack—you are displaying God's love.

You are validating that child's God-given worth.

You are doing something humble with great impact.

You are shaping the brain and heart of a human being.

This isn't just any old work. This is kingdom work when we do it with gospel-purpose.

Each Christlike action toward that infant is like a valuable jewel being placed in the treasure chest of the heart. The real investment doesn't begin later; the riches are adding up now.

It's not for us to say whether or not that child will someday notice and accept these riches available to them in Christ, but we can certainly help lay the best possible foundation for that child to later hear and receive the gospel.

So the next time you are with that sweet infant, make the little investments and trust God to do the rest. Your love matters because it points to the greatest love they can ever experience.

WHEN YOU'RE IN A RUT

EMILY

Sometimes in motherhood, I get into a rut. Days or weeks go by, and it's hard to turn everyday conversations into moments for pointing kids to Christ. The steady rumble of rambunctious voices makes it hard to fill the home with sounds of hymns, worship music, and prayers. The busy hour before dinner leads to half-hearted meals in front of the TV. Over time, these once exceptional things become the norm.

I understand ruts because we live in the country, near gravel roads. Ruts appear where vehicles have crossed the same path over and over again, making one section of the road smooth and easy to drive on. So much so that it's actually tough to drive on the bumpy portions and they almost force the tires of the car to the well-worn path.

So when I hit ruts in motherhood, especially ones I'm not happy about, I need to recognize that I'm going to have to actively think about breaking these habits. Just like those gravel roads, our brains' neurological connections form strong pathways to the things we've always done. Change might be bumpy for a while—but bumps aren't necessarily a sign that I'm doing something wrong.

We're women with old habits of sin learning to walk by the Spirit. We need to continually ask for the power to swerve away from the flesh and develop holy ruts. God can help us when it gets bumpy and things seem to get worse before they get better. He can hold our hands steady when discomfort sets in.

Holy ruts in motherhood fall in line with God's commands. They show a default toward patience, kindness, gentleness, and self-control—especially in the small things. They make it feel harder not to pray or give thanks. These ruts develop not by sheer determination but through our abiding dependence on God's Spirit.

What ruts have you fallen into lately? Will you pray, ask, and act—going out of the rut, through the bumps, and toward a life of holiness?

WHEN HOUSEWORK
FEELS POINTLESS

LAURA

It doesn't have to be just "vacuuming," "scrubbing," or "washing." When done in service to the Lord, with love and care and understanding that all is for the Lord, those old wood floors are not just floors—they're sacred ground. Hallowed. Because you are not just running a vacuum over the crumbs; you are offering worship to your God. When you as a mother recognize Christ is in all, then you are not merely "doing just a bit of housework"; you're imaging your Lord and Savior, offering a sacrifice of praise. His presence is there, right in that room. Recognize it—and you'll find the pathway to joy.

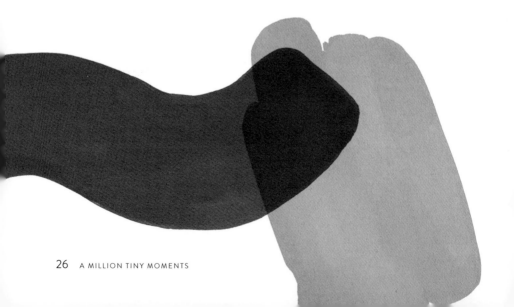

WHEN YOU
ARE WEARY

EMILY

When you're weary in motherhood and you feel like it's impossible to carry on in your current circumstances, let that be like a red flag waving in your life. Notice it, acknowledge it, and don't go running to your usual means of comfort—*extra coffee, more sweets, venting sessions with friends, more clothes added to cart, binge scrolling social media, yelling at your kids, and all of those other things that provide temporary relief.*

Run to Jesus. Pray. Humble yourself, and ask him for strength, wisdom, guidance, and love for your children. See how he might guide you with Scripture and through practical means of rest, help, and endurance.

God can and will equip you with everything you need for life and godliness through the Holy Spirit.

He can be your refuge, hiding place, strength, comforter, redeemer, and faithful guide in times of need. He is just waiting for you to stop going your own way and depend on the help made available to you through the sacrifice of Christ.

Be encouraged, because if you've placed your faith in Christ, then someday your Father will welcome you into his kingdom and tell you, "Well done." This good news is meant to give you hope to keep going in the midst of today's hardships.

FOR WHEN YOU
ARE AFRAID

——————

God is our strength, and he is by our side.
This doesn't mean that we stop walking or acting
or making decisions—but that we do it as we lean
into the Father's arms. We talk with God and
ask him to lead us all the way. Fears and trials
will come, but our Heavenly Father is with us.
Let's be moms who fixate on God's steadfast
love and faithfulness. In him, our souls are safe.

EMILY

WHEN OUR FEARS BECOME REAL

LAURA

What's so scary about our fears is the fact that so many of them could come true.

As moms, most of our fears revolve around our children and families. We want to protect our kids and give them the best lives we possibly can—to calculate every risk, provide for every need, to assess all possible outcomes to set them up for success.

But what happens when your kid has cancer, or your child was exposed to pornography, or your husband lost his job, or you have chronic pain and can't make dinner for your kids, or you live under the shadow of poor decisions your own parents made—then what?

These things might be true in your life. And it's true that they are scary. But what else is true is we serve the God whose footsteps thunder across earth, who set the boundaries of the sea behind doors and gave the dawn its place so it seizes the edges of the earth. Our God walks the depths of the oceans, holds lightning in his hands, and chains together the constellations in the night sky (Job 38).

All of this is more true and sure than the scary circumstances you face right now.

So here's the question: When life gets scary, what truth will win in your heart? What truth will ultimately triumph?

As women of God, we can be courageous in the knowledge that God has ordained all of our days, that he is always with us. The "boundary lines have fallen for [us] in pleasant places; indeed, [we] have a beautiful inheritance" (Psalm 16:6 csb). Our "help comes from the Lord, the Maker of heaven and earth" (Psalm 121:2 csb).

It's the Lord who protects us and keeps us in perfect peace as we call on him.

But here's the deal—we're not being asked to "never fear ever again." God is asking us to fear him *more*. Let's keep our fears in perspective because the scariest thing that could ever happen to us is being separated from God—and he's already protected us from that in Christ.

So things might get a lot more scary. We might lose popularity with other moms, we might make mistakes—even some major ones. Any number of hard things might happen to us and our children. But we can be moms who overcome fear with fear—the fear of the Lord can always triumph in our hearts because no matter what happens, we can trust in the character of God today and know that we have a secure, eternal inheritance and we will live forever with Christ.

This gives us courage over the scary circumstances in our lives.

Let's be moms who fear the Lord.

FOR THE WORST-CASE SCENARIO

EMILY

Although I try not to regularly dwell on or play out awful situations in my head, I've also experienced freedom as I've confronted my worst-case-scenario fears with gospel truth. The more I face the things I think my heart can't survive, the more I have faith in the promises of Christ. Even if my child's medical test comes back positive, my parent goes through having cancer, our business goes down the drain, or my child goes wayward, there are things that can never be taken from me.

No matter what happens, my future hope is unchanging.

Worst-case scenarios get their label for a reason—they're awful. Death, disease, empty bank accounts, public shame, or loss of relationships threaten our joy and plans for a good life. But God's definition of good is focused on his promises to his people. For instance, it's hard to think about, but God put what was likely Mary's worst-case scenario for motherhood (seeing her son, Jesus, publicly humiliated, tortured, and killed on a cross) at the center of history. But God was working in this awful thing for the redemption of his people. Paul acknowledged this mystery in his letter to the Philippians, noting that even in his imprisonment, God was doing good things because Paul had opportunities to spread the gospel. His suffering provided a chance to display contentment, trusting God's plans even when it defied earthly comfort.

When Peter writes a letter to the Christians in the dispersion, he tells them to praise God in the midst of their worst-case scenario. And it's not because things were going to eventually be wonderful for them on Earth but because things would ultimately be wonderful for them in heaven. They had a future hope that wasn't impacted by present tribulations.

In Christ, we share in this same hope and reward. Our present sufferings and worst-case-scenario fears can't be compared to the glory that is coming.

WHEN YOU FEEL INADEQUATE

LAURA

Inadequacy as a mother is one of my primary fears. When I think too deeply about the weight of my role as a mother, I easily get overwhelmed and feel scared that I'm not doing enough. That *I'm* not enough.

If you've been there too, remember this with me: While we are limited, we serve a God that is limitless. He knows all, sees all, is in all. He is not constrained by a mother's shortcomings; he is magnified in them. He is not hindered by inabilities; his fame is advanced because of them. He is not confined by weaknesses; he is proven strong in the midst of them.

Where a mother lacks, Christ is abundant.

So rest easy—for while you are limited, you serve a God who is completely, profoundly, radiantly limitless.

He can and will do great things through you, equipping you for every good work, with your children today and for eternity.

WHEN YOU KEEP FEELING AFRAID

EMILY

I'm learning that trusting God and giving my fears to him isn't a one-time decision—it's an ongoing posture and an outworking of my faith. I trust the Lord by continuing to pray, read Scripture, sing, give thanks, have fellowship with other believers, laugh, serve, and take the next step of obedience, even in hard and confusing times. I don't pretend to have this "fear" thing down just yet, but I'm growing in my ability to recognize when my decisions or reactions are rooted in the wrong kind of fear.

WHEN YOU FEEL EMBARRASSED

EMILY

For every mom, there comes a moment when your child embarrasses you. Big or small, in public or in the company of close friends, in an epic fallout or in a private "we need to talk about your child" meeting—it's bound to happen. Your cheeks flush, beads of sweat drip down your back, your throat clenches. Perhaps you laugh when you should be serious, or you're stern while everyone else laughs. Whatever your reaction, the pit in your stomach screams that people are watching, judging you and your child, finding you lacking.

Whether it was the times I lugged a screaming child to the car from the park, pool, or store; the outbursts of potty talk or rambunctious climbing in semiformal environments; or just the run-of-the-mill "I can't believe my kids are acting this way" events—I've had years of experience with this.

In my better moments, I debrief with my husband and kids and, most importantly, with the Lord. I pray and rehearse the narrative of the gospel and think on specific scriptures to process the situation. While there are numerous truths we might want or need to recall after moments of embarrassment in motherhood, here are three Bible truths to keep in mind.

Give Thanks

Give thanks in all circumstances; for this is the will of God in Christ Jesus for you.

1 THESSALONIANS 5:18

Even though we don't feel very thankful when little Johnny asks Aunt Marge why her tummy is so big and squishy, God's Word says there is always a reason to give thanks. Gratitude flows not only from good feelings but from a heart that believes God orchestrates, ordains, and provides challenging situations for our good. Sometimes we simply thank the Lord that we have children—even when caring for them means public tantrums and awkward interactions. Other times, we express gratitude for our salvation and identity in Christ, which defines us at all times, even when others don't approve of us or our children. And painfully, sometimes we give thanks for opportunities to see our children's foolishness, pride, or sin. While this doesn't seem like a gift, embarrassing moments can warn and remind us that we have a responsibility to train and discipline our children (Proverbs 29:15; Ephesians 6:4). The outburst of bad manners could mean that they need a nap (normal and understandable), or it could mean that we need to train them to love others and increase our discipleship in a specific area. No matter the cause of the embarrassment, it's always God's will for Christians to give him thanks.

Move Forward

Forgetting what lies behind and straining forward to
what lies ahead, I press on toward the goal for the
prize of the upward call of God in Christ Jesus.

PHILIPPIANS 3:13–14

When we're still cringing from the "talk" a neighborhood parent had with us about our child, most of us are ready to make a big ordeal of it or pretend it never happened. Neither of these responses are what Paul alludes to in his letter to the Philippians when he speaks about dealing with past sins and missteps as a believer. We seek to apologize, repent, and take responsibility when we've done something wrong, and we teach our children to do the same. Sometimes an embarrassing moment leads to an apology note or the loss of a privilege. But this verse particularly reminds our weary hearts that when we've been made right with God and we seek to live at peace with others to the best of our ability, there comes a time when we press on. We stop looking back again and again and again (replaying the situation or mulling it over), and instead, we look to Christ. We rehearse and remember our purpose and goal in motherhood instead of our embarrassing moment and point our kids to their Lord—the one who took all of their sin and shame on the cross. Because of our faith in Christ, there is always hope beyond embarrassing moments. Moms can move forward!

Don't Fear

The Lord is on my side; I will not fear. What can man do to me?

PSALM 118:6

This truth is so important, God repeated it throughout the Bible. It's one that we need in many situations, but is helpful to remember when an embarrassing moment leaves us feeling fearful of others' opinions. Perhaps it's when a child with special needs makes socially abnormal noises and gestures in a quiet environment or when you hear from a teacher that your child struggles to read aloud (when their peers are right on track). Even though no one sinned, you still feel like you should have done better for your child, or you grieve the challenges they face and the way these impact relationships. In this, we can take heart because the Lord is tender with those who are weak and brokenhearted. For those who are his in Christ, he is on our side. He is for us now and in eternity. Nothing can separate us from his love—not even an embarrassing parenting moment (Romans 8:38-39). We might have socially outcast moments in motherhood, but in Christ, God will never cast us out. While our son or daughter might not get an invitation to the party or be included in the special club, we can be confident that this doesn't have to determine the course of eternity. People have the ability to leave one another out of groups, but they don't have the ability to leave others out of heaven.

If you're sweating an embarrassing moment in motherhood, it's good to debrief. Think through what happened—maybe next time, you'll pack an extra snack or special pack of stickers in your purse. Lesson learned! Perhaps there is something deeper at play, and you need to have a conversation about kind words and respectful behavior in different settings. Maybe everything was totally out of your control, and you're further reminded that your children belong to the Lord—you can do your best to mother them in his ways, but you can't help the decisions they make! Regardless of the details, these truths can hopefully be an encouragement to you. Find a reason to thank the Lord, keep pressing on in your walk with him, and fear him first.

WHEN MOTHERHOOD
FEELS HEAVY

LAURA

There's this thing I've noticed when you become a mom. It happens abruptly, beginning with the first night of the first babe, yet I'd be willing to bet that most moms don't even notice it happening. It's subtle—a common thread among all of motherhood, but one that would rather not be noticed, not be plucked out and put on display.

As moms, we spend most of our time looking down. We look down at the soup for supper, down at the toys our toddler left for us to trip over, down at our baby's gums, inspecting them for teeth. We look down to scrub the floors, to fill the bottles, to fix the broken scooter, to chop the food into tiny, bite-sized pieces. We look down to read the ingredients on the food packaging, learn the latest research on vaccines, and check the boxes on progress reports at the doctor's office. We look down because, as moms, our lives tend to run below us.

Yet we look down not only on things but on people. We look down on other moms for the way they feed, diaper, sleep train, and discipline their babies. We look down on how they dress, how they talk, and how they spend their time or money.

And at the same time, we find it pretty easy to look down on ourselves. To look down on how our days went, how dinner turned out, or how we didn't get enough "me time." We look down on our mothering skills, kicking ourselves for not doing enough intentional activities with our kids or not keeping our homes tidy enough, keeping our tempers long enough, or measuring up to those other mothers we just finished looking down on.

And lately, I've been feeling like I have a bit of a crick in my neck. Looking down at life and people and myself, my neck and shoulders and head all ache from the effort.

Mama, are you tired too? Is your neck bent and stiff from looking down?

Motherhood is good at weighing heavy on our shoulders. Turning us closed and inward, shuffling through all the questions, decisions, must-dos, should-dos, gotta-dos. There's a constant inward battle of acting like a self-sufficient know-it-all while at the same time doubting our every move and feeling like one big, giant failure.

And that's because we're only looking down.

Look up.

Look up and see the big, grand picture of motherhood. Look up and realize that motherhood isn't really about all those things you spend so much mental and physical energy on. It's not about finding the perfect eat-sleep-play schedule, the magic bullet to keeping your nursing supply, raising a musical prodigy, or getting the perfect schooling solution.

Motherhood is about the gospel.

Look up and see the cross. Look up and find that the work you are doing matters eternally. Look up and remember that you are not raising a body—you are raising a soul. Look up and remember that it has all been done before and there is nothing new that you are struggling with. You are not alone.

Look up and see how small and insignificant those things that hold your head down really are. Look up and see how you are loved and treasured. Look up and show others the love and grace you have received. Look up and cling to the cross.

Today, turn your face from the ground to the sky. Get outside of your research, your need for answers, your desire to "get it all right." Stop the comparing, the judgment, the criticism, and remember what motherhood is about: showing our children the love of Jesus and resting in his grace.

Look up.

FOR WRESTLING
WITH THE ENEMY

_____

EMILY

As hard as it is to recognize at times, the dirty dishes are not your enemy.

Your enemy is not your child's bad attitude or your husband's habits. Your enemy is not your flourishing friends or that "perfect" mom on social media. It isn't even the personal weaknesses that seem to give you endless grief.

Ephesians 6:12 says this about our enemies: "For we do not wrestle against flesh and blood, but against the rulers, against the authorities, against the cosmic powers over this present darkness, against the spiritual forces of evil in the heavenly places."

Mama, we must pause and remember that our enemies are real but may not be what they seem. The spiritual forces of evil want you to avoid this: looking to Christ, remembering who he is and what he's done for you, and joyfully passing along this hope to others.

The enemy is fine with you doing outwardly good things, as long as you're not looking at the best thing—Jesus Christ and his unchanging Word. He's fine with you giving anything to your children, except for hope in Christ. He's fine with you doing your work in any way, except as an offering of worship to God.

This week, reconsider your weapons and where they should be pointed. Fight your real enemies by believing the Word of God and cultivating a relationship with the One who will bring you eternal joy. Arm yourself with the gospel—believe it, look at the beauty of the Savior, and be a mama ready for battle because you're clothed in his righteousness.

FOR THE DANGER
WE CAN'T SEE

EMILY

While a child sees a tiny plastic block on the floor, shrugs, and shoves it into his mouth, a mom sees the choking hazard. Asking the child to spit it out isn't harsh; it's helpful. A mom can do this because she's lived longer, she knows more, and she has authority.

When a child clicks around on every website link to find the next funny video, a mom knows there is serious danger for both heart and mind lurking behind the wrong click. Taking away the device or setting up firm boundaries isn't being unfairly restrictive—it's trying to give the child a life without bondage to violent or pornographic images.

From a mother's point of view, it's easy to nod along and say, "Absolutely, mom knows best!" But what about when we're the child? Our Heavenly Father, who loves his children more than we can even understand, spends a lot of time warning us in his Word, trying to instill the right kind of fear in our hearts. But do we listen? Or do we assume he's being unfair, unkind, and restrictive?

He's not just lived longer—he's existed forever. He's the Alpha and the

Omega, the beginning and the end. He doesn't just know more than us; he knows everything. Even the number of hairs on our heads! He's not being unfair or unkind—he has authority, and he wants us to know the dangers that lie outside of his will, his ways, his presence, and his purposes. He wants us to know that the wicked have no future and that walking in sin is more dangerous than sprinting into a busy intersection.

When we read the Bible, we can respond as we hope our own children do when we give them warnings. We can stop and turn to God with a heart ready to obey. His words are trustworthy, pure, righteous, and reliable. They can make us wise—showing us paths that lead to danger. They can leave our saddened hearts glad, our tired legs strong, and our frantic minds quieted.

Because we're unable to see and know all the dangerous things in this life, we need the warnings of God's Word. We need to know what and whom to fear in this life and the next. Not all fear is bad. In fact, fear of the Lord and obedience to his ways are just what we need, and that type of fear is something to be grateful for.

WHEN YOU NEED TO KNOW GOD IS WITH YOU

EMILY

A mother's comfort often comes in the form of an embrace. When a child faces a fear or shares a deep insecurity, she kneels down, wrapping her arms around the child's shoulders. Her tight squeeze and lowered posture communicate, "Mom loves you. Mom is with you." With this gesture, the child can have peace again. The circumstances might not change, but the child is also not alone. Her stronger, wiser, caring parent is by her side.

We often don't think of the nativity scene as equal to a parental hug, but it should be a similar comfort to God's children. In the midst of our sin, fear, and shame, Christ came down. "He emptied himself by assuming the form of a servant, taking on the likeness of humanity" (Philippians 2:7 CSB). Figuratively, he came to our side—stooping low to make a way for us to be with him forever, through his atoning death and resurrection. After he rose again, he sent us a Helper: the Holy Spirit. All of this culminates into a promise of life—that through Christ, we might enter God's presence and be by his side forever.

This promise is the squeeze that comforts our souls in times of trouble. His help and presence, both now and forever, give us hope in the face of fear. God doesn't wrap us in a physical embrace, but he holds us securely through the Son. Through Christ, we can know that God is on and by our side.

For the mom wading through tough conversations with a hard-hearted child—God is with you. For the mom who struggles as she fits in less and less with her friends—God is with you.

For the mom who entrusts her child into the care of others while she's at work—God is with you.

For the mom trying to love with long-suffering through an ailing marriage—God is with you.

God is our strength, and he is by our side. This doesn't mean that we stop walking or acting or making decisions—but that we do it as we lean into the Father's arms. We talk with God and ask him to lead us all the way.

Fears and trials will come, but our Heavenly Father is with us.

WHEN THE WORLD FEELS SCARY

LAURA

Sometimes, the world feels scary. Watching the news or scrolling social media, many of us mothers find ourselves asking, "What kind of world have I brought my children into?" and "What can I do about it?"

It might not feel like there is much you can do, but actually, you can do a lot. You can raise your children to weep for a loss of life. To have mercy on the helpless. To know that all people are created in the image of God and every life matters. You can teach your children to have eyes for the hurting, hands for helping, and hearts of courage. You can teach them what it means to have a deep conviction for truth, paired with mercy and empathy for lost and hurting souls.

If you want to see your world changed, then start with your own children.

When you talk to your children in the car about loving people different from you and not placing stereotypes on them, you teach them how to love the sojourner. When you treat people you don't understand with respect and love in front of your children, you teach them mercy and compassion.

When your children watch you swing by a birth center to stand up for a helpless baby in the womb's right to life, you show them what it looks like to fight for truth. When you email your politicians, serve on the PTA, or walk to the mailbox to send money to a cause you care about, you teach them what it means to be a deep thinker and high-action taker, shaped by a love for what God loves.

You, Mama, are enormously, vitally part of the cause to change the world.

In everything you do, every bedtime story, every breakfast conversation, every walk to the park or drop-off at daycare, you shape them to someday change the world.

Our children are taught not in lengthy, eloquent speeches or in a few random moments of awkward talk about Christian values—no, they are shaped and transformed little by little, through living life with you each day.

You want to know what you can do about the scary news today?

You can start by modeling Jesus to your children right now.

FOR WHEN YOU
NEED GOOD NEWS

Jesus has seen everything you are,
knows everything, and still loves you,
Mom. Just think about that for a bit.

LAURA

WHEN YOU WANT TO KNOW YOU'RE A GOOD MOM

EMILY AND LAURA

"Am I a good mom?" seems to be the essential question of motherhood. It rings in our ears as we read books on the couch, knead dough on the counter, and sign our kids up for camps. It blares in our brains when we forget the permission slip for school, when we yell "Hurry up!" and when we fail to address a discipline issue.

We size ourselves up to the standards of Christian-mom culture. We measure ourselves by tangible progress. (If we don't make the first goal, maybe we can make the second?) It seems we're always grasping, reaching, striving. "Good mom" is as elusive as what our kids want for dinner. It changes depending on our mood, our experiences, those around us, and what we're watching and reading.

So how can we know? How can we answer the question, "Am I a good mom?"

If we're honest, we all know we're not always good moms. There are moments where we're forgetful or unorganized, and sometimes we have bursts of anger or struggle with selfishness. We might do good for a bit, but then we mess up. So we try again. And fail again. Deep down, the guilt always seems to remain.

Jesus knew this about us. He knew we couldn't meet God's standard for holiness in motherhood—or any area of life. For this, we are even guiltier than we feel. So Jesus came to meet the standard and be the sacrifice for us. In him, we can be declared (as mankind was in Eden) "very good."

True goodness comes from putting our faith in and giving our allegiance to Jesus. Christ is the only one who was perfectly good, and he gave us his good record by grace through faith.

His goodness makes us good, so we can do good.

For the Christian mom, doing good doesn't mean "being perfect" on this side of heaven, but it does mean living and loving like Christ with God's help day by day.

So, Mom, the "essential question" isn't really "Are you a good mom?" The "essential question" is, "Do you know and love the One who makes you good?"

Your answer to that question is the one that matters for all you do in life and motherhood.

BECAUSE NOTHING IS FREE

EMILY

My husband and I like to tell our kids that nothing is really free. It's a concept they challenge when we're out and about—especially while standing at the counter of a local small business, loading their pockets with tootsie rolls. Or there is that gum from grandma's car console, or the stickers and temporary tattoos handed out at the parade, or the books that came home from the library.

"See, Mom? These are free!"

"But are they? Who paid for this?" I'll ask later in the car. A rare silence settles on every seat.

No matter how "free" something feels, it always costs someone something. We can trace it back to a business owner, a family member, a neighbor, or a taxpayer. Even acts of service and love cost someone time, physical energy, financial resources, and personal sacrifice.

This is the paradigm of the gospel—grace cost someone everything.

While we were dead in our sin, lining our pockets with tootsie rolls and mucking about the swamp of selfishness, Christ came to save us. He lived the life we should have lived and died the death we should have died—he took the punishment for our sin at the cost of his very life. We can't even really comprehend what he paid, but he paid in full.

So while grace is a free gift to us, it wasn't free for Christ. This realization shouldn't discourage or deflate us—it should sober us. Temper our hearts and actions. Cause us to savor this life and the gifts we've been given. To receive all things with thanksgiving.

But the transformation of our hearts doesn't end there! This attitude—knowing that our lives come at a great cost to Christ—causes us to be generous with others. We become more and more willing to give people our love, time, resources, prayers, and personal attention, even when it's costly. We look at Christ's ministry and see that it wasn't free, so ours won't be either.

The service we do in motherhood isn't free. There is a cost to our bodies, our hearts, our minds, our sleep patterns, and our schedules. But generous love is a way we can show our kids and communities the free gift of grace we have because of Christ's sacrifice.

FOR APPLYING THE GOSPEL

EMILY

Being a Christian affects every part of motherhood. We're *Christian* moms when we read a board book to our baby, who just wants to eat the pages. We're *Christian* moms when we're in the doctor's office, receiving news of a miscarriage. We're *Christian* moms when we hear a tough report from a schoolteacher about our child's progress. We're *Christian* moms when we interact with the nanny. Christian moms receive and respond to all things— big and small, amazing and mundane, easy and horrific—in light of the good news of what Jesus Christ has done for them and who he's called them to be.

This means that no matter the circumstances, we can apply the truths of the gospel.

We can consider God's design for his creation as laid out in the Bible.

We can consider the Fall and sin's effects on mankind.

We can turn to Christ and consider his life and work on our behalf.

We can live by the power of the Spirit through the guidance of God's Word.

We can look to the future with hope, knowing that no matter what happens, Christ will return and make all things new.

The Gospel Has Power to Change Us

All of life and motherhood are impacted by our identity and hope in Christ, and this, by the Spirit's work, changes us. As we remember the story of our salvation through Christ, realize what it bought us, and receive it with joy, we are changed (Romans 1:16). We see this in the lives of people that Jesus encountered, including the apostles and early converts. Murderers became evangelists. Fishermen and tax collectors became preachers. Pagans who worshipped false gods became followers of Yahweh and suffered for Christ. It's the application of the gospel that moment by moment, prayer by prayer, conflict by conflict focuses our hearts more fully on Christ (2 Corinthians 3:18). As a sculptor once said about his project, "I just chip away everything that doesn't look like an elephant." We're women who are being conformed to Christ, and the gospel message is a main way that we're chiseled into his image (Romans 8:29).

But the Gospel Doesn't Immediately Solve Everything

In some ways, the gospel is a story of an immediate fix. After all, Christ died once for all sins (Romans 6:10). We don't have to grovel or say the "magic words" (pretty-pretty please!) to get him to forgive us. When we repent of sin and turn to him in faith, we're justified (Romans 5:1)! We're righteous. It's finished. But life after the Fall and before the final return of Christ means that we will still struggle and suffer and sin. We might apply the gospel at 9:00 a.m. and then again at 9:15. We might have an ongoing struggle in our relationship with our husband or have a child with a disability that won't necessarily be "cured" in this life. We'll be frustrated if we think "applying the gospel" will make all our pain go away in this life, even the pain we feel when we look at our own failures. The gospel story itself shows us that the presence of sin and impacts of the Fall will persist until Christ's return. Our Christian walk is about depending on God, rejoicing in his grace day by day until we die.

Maybe you blew it right before you read this entry. Maybe it was this morning, or maybe it will be five minutes from now. Maybe you're processing some difficult news, or you're sad over a child's ongoing disobedience. Whatever it is—related to sin or just the general griefs and struggles we face in life—apply the gospel again and again. It's a normal and encouraging mark of a believer to feel grieved by our sin and repeatedly turn back to Christ. Our obedience brings glory to God, and gospel application produces growth—even if it's slower than the tree in your backyard! God will work through his Spirit and Word in your life to bring you joy in him and wisdom in your situation, even if your problems and sins aren't magically gone. He is always with you.

WHEN CHRIST IS OUR SOURCE OF JOY

EMILY

Did you know that finding joy in Christ frees us up to enjoy other things? When people don't have to bear the weight of our good feelings and expectations, they can just be what they are—image-bearers, sinners, gifts from God. We can laugh when they do something funny, ask them tough questions when we think they might be in error, give praise when they do something great, and smile at the pleasure of our relationship with them.

People aren't a threat to our joy when they aren't the source of it.

WHEN YOU NEED NEW LIFE

EMILY

When we purchased our first home, I couldn't get past the wallpaper. It was velvety and flocked, not changed or updated in 40+ years. Although the previous owners had taken care of many structural aspects of the home, they had barely maintained anything cosmetic.

The house smelled, the stone fireplace was coated in dust and soot, the carpet was matted and worn, and the light fixtures could barely function under a layer of greasy dirt. Someone had obviously decorated it once, never to be touched again.

We stripped everything from the walls, floors, and ceilings, nearly gutting the place. We scraped, scrubbed, polished, and restored. We built the stories of our early married days as we argued amidst wood-floor installation and loud tile saws. Months later, it was finished, and that dirty, dingy house was a bright, fresh space that would later become a home for our young children.

Looking back, one thing I learned is that remodeling can be a picture of taking something with no life, no hope, and no future and giving it just that.

And this reminds me of the gospel—what God does for us, who need more than some surface updates but are completely dead in our trespasses. When there was nothing we could do to save ourselves or shape up, he died on the cross and gave us new hearts, a new future, a bright shining hope, and a commission to love others with the love and mercy he's shown us.

So whether you do a full-home remodel, spruce up a bathroom, or give an old piece of furniture new life, you can use these examples to talk to others (your children included) about what God does for us in the gospel. Each time people enjoy that restored thing or space, hopefully a little thought can come to mind about God's grace and mercy, bringing dead things to life again.

FOR THE MORNING

LAURA

What if you woke up each morning and thought,
"I am saved from my sins,
I have all that Christ has,
and I'm going to heaven someday."
How would that change your days?

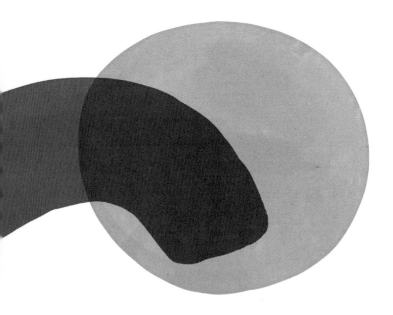

WHEN YOU HAVE HIGH STANDARDS

EMILY

Sometimes our hopes and expectations for our mothering are so high, we find ourselves regularly despairing over the ways we fail.

Everything we do can become an effort to achieve our version of a perfect family life—eating the right foods, participating in the right activities, keeping the right level of clean, dressing our kids in the right clothes, and using the right type of toys.

But devotion to our version of a "perfect family" will never yield the joy we long for. It will always leave us needing to do more and more and more to finally get it right.

The good news is that you can stop posturing, as you've been made perfect through the righteousness of Christ because of his sacrifice. Let this scandal and wonderful gospel reality propel you to do good works and love your family well from a heart of joy.

FOR REMEMBERING
YOUR IDENTITY IN CHRIST

EMILY

Live long enough, and you'll find yourself a label. Some have been placed there by others (names we were called as children, rumors spread about us in high school, praises we've received), and some we've placed on ourselves (sin patterns we fall into, mantras we repeat in our heads, ideas about who we think we should be). We naturally link ourselves to labels, and those labels have power.

This happens in motherhood too. Instead of viewing ourselves as God does, we tend to latch on to words and phrases that we feel define us as moms. Over time, we start to see ourselves through the lens of "Mary, the angry mom," or "Julie, the messy person," or "Kayla, the type A over-achiever." And the more we repeat and believe these labels, the more we live up to them. It's a vicious cycle. Our identities are linked to our behaviors. *Who we are, who we think we are,* or *who we want to be* often determine *what we do* and *how we live.*

The power of personal identity is one of the main reasons God spends so much of the Bible telling us who we were created to be, who we are in him, who we are apart from him, and who we become in Christ. It's why he lays out his design for us as image-bearers, reassures us of his love and faithfulness, and places our belonging firmly in his care.

When we forget who we are in Christ—redeemed, unashamed, clean, full of hope, heirs of wonderful promises with access to God—and we only see ourselves as sinners, mad mamas, trying-so-hard-to-please-him wives, laid-back failures, used-to-sleep-around women, always-accomplishing-everything employees, organic-food moms, homeschoolers, and so on, we become ruled by those labels instead of Christ. We live unto them instead of him. From those identities (and we like to wear several at once), we try hard, we hide, we posture, and we sulk away from the Father who loves us.

This is why many New Testament letters repeat the gospel, taking great care to remind us of the wonderful good news that we are dead to sin and alive in Christ, because who we are in him speaks truth over all our other identities. From the basis of who we are in Christ, we love differently, we look out for the interests of others, we stand on truth, we forgive, we submit, and we pursue peace. We are not "angry moms" trying to get our tempers under control—we are redeemed and righteous image-bearers who still wrestle with sin in the process of becoming more like Jesus while we wait for our final restoration.

God tells us who we are in Christ—not because we have arrived today but because we will arrive when we meet Christ. The more we believe that—remembering our identity in Christ *today*—the more we can cast off lies and walk in the way we'll walk for eternity.

So the next time you hear someone say, "Just remember your identity in Christ," you can know what it means: Even though right now it feels like you can't do anything right—like you are discouraged and tired of the way you continually blow it when you try to do the right thing—sin no longer defines you. Don't start condemning yourself; remember the whole truth: You are now a saint. You are clean. You are redeemed. You are waiting for the full restoration that is coming. You have the power of the Holy Spirit in you. No one can tarnish that or take it away.

However you think of it, let it be a reminder that you are a new creation in Christ, which is definitely a label worth remembering.

WHEN YOU JUST WANT TO
HEAR YOU'RE DOING A GOOD JOB

LAURA

We all want to be good mothers. We all want to hear our friends and family turn and whisper in our ears, "You're doing a good job, Mom."

And there is nothing wrong with that, as long as it's put in its proper place. Because sometimes, we can be so desperate to hear those words that we place our hope in them. This leads to us living our lives in an unsatisfied and burdened way, trying to keep up with the world's ever-changing standards of what the world says "good moms" do.

Your strengths and successes in motherhood can't define you or give you purpose. Though it's tempting to think this way, your significance can't be based on how you school your children, how you clean and feed them, or how you nurture their musical skills. It can't be found in how you dress, or how you clean the house, or how you always have just the right thing to say.

When you focus too much on these things—when all you want to hear is someone tell you "You're doing a good job"—you'll always feel insecure in who you are.

Thankfully, we are called not to boast in the flesh but to boast in the cross: "But far be it from me to boast except in the cross of our Lord Jesus Christ, by which the world has been crucified to me, and I to the world" (Galatians 6:14).

Because Christ paid your debt on the cross, you always have God's approval and acceptance. He declares you "good" all the time in his sight. And when you realize that, the opinions and expectations of others don't control you: not the latest fad, not your current circumstances, not what the news says, and not how your friends and family think you should mother. Nothing but God's Word can tell you what to do.

Boasting in the cross remembers that the world *can't give* you anything you don't already have, and it *can't take* anything from you that you actually need.

When you boast in the cross, the world's expectations don't hold power over you. You are free to be who you are in Christ. Free to be joyful, free to be at peace, free to be an individual, unique mom to your children. You can live unaffected by the world around you because all you have is already found in Christ.

So today, let God's voice be the one you hear. Because of Jesus, God's approval of you never changes. He is all you need. He is the only thing worth boasting about.

FOR WHEN
YOU ARE LIMITED

———————

The other day I asked God, "Lord, what can
I do for you that will matter for eternity?
I'll do anything!" I thought, "I'll be a missionary.
I'll go work for church. I'll even give all my
money away."

But do you want to know what the Spirit
brought to mind? "Be patient with your husband.
Be kind with your children. Be a good neighbor."

I was ready to turn my life upside down,
but what the Spirit asked was that I simply be
faithful in the life he's already given me.

LAURA

WHEN YOU HIT YOUR LIMIT

EMILY

Sometimes we want to be a supermom—meeting every need, staying up extra late, getting up super early, trying harder, problem-solving better, taking on more of the load, or researching more thoroughly. But as we serve our families with our energy and efforts, at some point, even the highest-capacity mom hits a wall and finds her limit. When we think we can spin everything and the plates fall, we call it our failure. But what if we were never meant to be the plate spinner? What if the world is not ours to control, uphold, and supply?

God is the only one who is all-knowing, all-powerful, and ever-present. He formed every mountain, gave the seas their boundaries, and knows the number of hairs on every head. He upholds the world by the word of his power. He is Lord of all.

We are created in his image as women with human needs and limitations. We're finite. We can't be in all places at all times or be all things to all people. We aren't meant to do life alone or be completely sufficient in and of ourselves. The fact that we are "not enough" and can't fix every problem isn't a flaw in God's design; it's his intention. When we recognize we're not supposed to be God, we can experience freedom and humbly run to him for help.

Acknowledging your ultimate and deep need for God and his grace doesn't mean you instantly have all your problems fixed. In fact, biblical wisdom tells us to ask others for help and support. You can still ask a friend to start a meal train, reach out to a doctor or counselor for help, ask another family member to take your child to therapy, or get more frequent childcare or a house cleaner for a season.

We can't spin every plate in motherhood because we were never designed to. Depend wholly on the Lord, ask for his help, and see what he would have you care for by his strength. As you go about your day, keep looking for the practical ways that God provides for your needs.

WHEN YOU CAN'T SEEM TO GET IT TOGETHER

LAURA

Today, I'm reminded of how far I am from being a good mother, friend, wife, daughter, church member, volunteer—a good anything! I want to do better. I just can't seem to get it together. At times, it can feel pretty bleak. Why can I not live out what I know to be true? If I have Christ, why do I sometimes feel lost? If I know his promises are true, why do I act like they don't exist?

And so when I'm exasperated, when I'm shocked by my own sin, when I am at the end of my rope, I stop, remember the cross, and sing,

I need Thee, oh, I need Thee; Every hour I need Thee.

I sing it so much, my son sings this song to me when he thinks I'm sad. With a tentative voice two keys higher than mine, he'll look right at me and sing,

I need Thee, oh, I need Thee; Every hour I need Thee.

I can't do it on my own because I was never meant to. I need Christ to sustain me, not my own efforts. Every day, every hour, every minute, he gives me my very life. And the beautiful thing is he doesn't just sustain me with the bare minimum—no, he fills me with life abundantly! He gives me all I need in every moment.

If you're like me, your story is a story of someone who needs her Savior every hour, who wrestles with doing bad and doing good and finds the gospel right in the middle of the struggle.

We need Thee, oh, we need Thee; Every hour we need Thee.

BECAUSE WE ORBIT AROUND CHRIST, NOT OUR KIDS

EMILY

I understand the feeling of wanting to give it all for my children because I've seen the temporary look of elation on their faces when they're holding out for sprinkle-covered donuts. For a moment, it seems the power of the domestic universe resides in a box of fried, sugary dough. The key to bribery, kind words, joyful children, and mommy worship is in my hands. I understand what it feels like to pass out the second or third round of treats, feeling proud satisfaction because I made my children happy (and quiet), all with an inexpensive sugary delight. But soon after, the bribe betrays me as those quiet, frosting-covered mouths inevitably turn sour. My efforts are in vain. I have given a good gift, but I have not given enough to fill their endless chasm of want.

The "Give It All" Myth

You see, when I give everything I have for my children, there are some temporal rewards and immediate pleasures. When I offer my gifts, service, time, effort, money, and love on the altar of parenthood, for a moment, there is peace. The smiles abound. The laughter increases. Satisfaction appears to be secured. In a good scenario, I occasionally hear, "Thank you, Mommy!" and even better, the spontaneous "I love you." But it's never enough for them, or for me.

Doesn't this type of parental sacrifice seem rational? Because we love our children, we should also give it all for them, right? This is certainly a popular idea in our culture. Our children's birthdays and holidays abound with monumental traditions and heaps of presents. They are rarely without entertainment, activity, socialization, and internet-capable devices. We think our children are deserving of only the finest athletic and academic training. They take our sleep at will, our nerves over time, our public acclaim in an instant, and our rational minds when we're not looking. But we don't notice because we're busy handing out donuts. We're just doing our best to give it all for their sake.

The "If You Want to Love Well, Give It All for Jesus" Myth

The thing is, Jesus doesn't tell us to give it all for our children. He says that we are to give it all to him and hate everyone else *in comparison* to how much we love and treasure him (Luke 14:26). That's uncomfortable for us to hear, but it's an important principle to take with us into motherhood. It means that Christ, not our children, reigns supreme in our lives.

Would this mean we ignore their needs, feed them unhealthy foods, give them terrible gifts, and neglect all responsibility for various types of training? Absolutely not. Giving our all to Jesus should motivate us to love our children in a radical way. Giving it all for our children will ultimately let us down when they fail to give us adequate affection, gratitude, obedience, and achievements. We might give it all for our children, but they will never repay our efforts. But there is a person who outdoes our efforts. A man who goes before us, who gave it all for our salvation, and who holds our eternal reward secure.

Culture is telling you that if you just do enough, give enough, and get it right enough, then you will reap a due reward for your good parenting. But if you want to give really good, eternally significant gifts to your children, become poor in spirit, take up your cross, walk in freedom from sin, and be willing to do whatever Jesus asks of you in this life. He will undoubtedly ask you to love unselfishly with a long-suffering heart and a desire to do what is best for those in your care. He will ask you to provide for your children, nurture their hearts, and give them grace that points to the Redeemer.

For future reference, if you catch me giving my kids donuts, it's not primarily so I can obtain their praise. It's because I'm teaching them the value of enjoying all things for God's glory out of a heart that is ultimately allegiant to Jesus. Oh, and it's because I'm free to give them too much sugar (at least sometimes).

WHEN YOU DOUBT YOU'RE GOOD ENOUGH

EMILY

As moms, we are each going to bloom a little differently—becoming lovely as we root ourselves in truth and drink the living water that only Jesus can provide. As each mom joyfully seeks to love Christ, love her family well, and share the gospel, she will uniquely bless those around her.

But too often, we doubt that the way we flower is good.

Instead, we compare ourselves to other moms and issue harsh judgments according to the standards of the microculture we're in.

We start to feel like "good moms" must bloom a certain way…

They must throw *these* types of birthday parties.

They must not serve *those* snacks.

They must lose the weight in *this* amount of time.

They must choose *this* type of schooling.

They must not provide *that* type of toy.

They must discipline in *this* type of way.

And on, and on, and on…

The standards vary by era, culture, geographic location, and socio-economic status, but oh, they exist!

As moms who follow Jesus, we get to do motherhood God's way. We don't live in bondage to the expectations of those around us. We are free to obey the Lord and how he is leading us.

Free to live for God's glory, even when it looks different from our friends.

Free to share Christ in ways that reflect our giftings.

Free to love others in ways that fit the situation.

Free to make choices from a heart of faith.

Free to resist the desires of our flesh for our selfish gain.

So, Mama…how are you trying to measure up to the moms around you? How can you stop judging and start blooming exactly how God created you to?

And how can you enjoy the beauty of the garden, appreciating God's design for the spread of the gospel through a variety of fragrant blooms?

WHEN YOU NEED GRATITUDE

EMILY

I dragged my dishrag along the countertop for the third time that day with a forced smile.

Recently, I'd heard that smiling could impact my body and my mood. Apparently, the physical act of turning up the corners of my lips and clinching the apples of my cheeks emits "happy" brain chemicals that can lower my cortisol levels and reduce my heart rate. Experts say this effect also extends to the recipient of a smile. I thought I'd try it.

We don't have many biblical details about Jesus's facial expressions as he ministered here on earth, but we do know that he obeyed his Father with a glad and contented heart. We can observe that he experienced a range of human emotions at the right times. He expressed happiness when it was time to rejoice, spoke pointed words when it was time for a rebuke, and wept when it was time to mourn. Because of his humility, he served and obeyed the Father with a glad heart.

And as moms, the best type of service doesn't come from our forced smiles—even if God's grace by design allows us to experience its positive physical effects. We need to observe the One who deserved everything but laid his life down for the joy set before him. Scripture directs tired people who struggle with their entitlement to "consider him who endured from sinners such hostility against himself, so that you may not grow weary or fainthearted" (Hebrews 12:3). When we consider Jesus, we're led to gratitude, worship, reverence, and awe.

It's this type of gratitude that produces true gladness. It's God's work that produces worship in our work. It's reverence and awe that move our hands, our dishrags, and even our lips to turn up into a smile.

BECAUSE AGE OFTEN GIVES WAY TO BEAUTY

EMILY

There's not an age limit on fearing the Lord. In fact, I think that in God's kind of economy of beauty, the older someone gets, the more perhaps they may fear the Lord—the more they may grow in peace and joy and self-control and patience and Christlikeness. As you age, if you are walking with Christ, you're becoming more and more and more beautiful, not less.

WHEN YOU DON'T
FEEL BEAUTIFUL

LAURA

Everyone has been given a different measure of physical beauty. It's true that some people are more physically beautiful than others. Scripture points this out with Esther, David, Sarah, and others who are noted as beautiful or good-looking. And Scripture specifically notes that Jesus had no beauty that would attract us to him (Isaiah 53:1). Just like God does with other things like skills, talents, and money, God grants physical beauty as a gift to some people more than others. Since all of us at times struggle to varying degrees with our appearance, it can help if we can keep in mind a few biblical truths when we look in the mirror.

Our bodies (and their beauty) are not a measure of our value or worth. What makes us worthy is that we were made in the image of God—and that never changes or fades. He intricately wove your body together in the womb and specifically gave you your elbows, nose, and toes. No matter your age, abilities, or whether you feel beautiful or "good in your skin" as a mother, your value is rooted and secure.

What makes us more like Christ is also often what physically ages our bodies. Science tells us that the symptoms of grief and motherhood—sleeplessness, stress, inflammation, physical illness, and so on—all increase the effects of physical aging. But because we live in an upside-down kingdom, suffering is actually what makes us more beautiful in our souls, as God uses it to eradicate sin and soften our hearts to be more like his. While our bodies are decaying on the outside, they're being renewed on the inside.

Christ shows us that we don't need to be beautiful to be effective for the kingdom. Going back to point number one—if a stunning physical appearance were crucial to the mission of the visible image of the invisible God, then Christ would have had it—and he didn't. If beauty wasn't essential for our Lord, it's not essential for us.

It's okay to desire to feel beautiful. God designed all of humanity to have an appreciation and admiration of beautiful things. Our desire to feel beautiful is a reflection of how he made us. And like with other desires we have (to be known, loved, in community, etc.), it points to the reality of being made by and for God and how, because of Jesus's sacrifice, we are beautiful in God's sight.

It's normal to want to feel and look young. Not because of some evolutionary development for fertility, but because we were actually *made* to be eternal and live in perfect bodies in heaven with God forever. This world is a stop on the way to our final destination, and we can feel it.

WHEN YOU FEEL LIKE YOU "SHOULD" EXERCISE

LAURA

Over my years as a mom, my level of physical exercise has ebbed and flowed. After birthing each child, my physical activity was nonexistent. For the large majority of my days, I was sedentary, sleeping and sitting as a baby's warm cheek rested on my chest. Movement in that season looked like rocking in a chair, bouncing a colicky baby, and tiptoeing out the door of the room of a sleeping toddler. And this was right and good. But if you're like me, eventually, as the hazy newborn days clear and something like a schedule falls into place, you start to think about how and why you might fit exercise and movement into your mom life.

Sometimes, it's because we want to lose a few pounds, and other times it's simply because we know it can bring on mood-boosting endorphins. (Who doesn't want those?) And while these reasons aren't necessarily wrong, there's a difference between conforming our bodies to an Instagram post and moving them in order to be strong, healthy, and able to do the work required for life and motherhood. Genesis 1:21 tells us that God made living creatures to move—that life and movement go together. God didn't make us trees or plants, stationary life rooted to the ground—no, his creatures are to walk and run and jump.

Movement is one grand way God designed humans to image and glorify him—and that's the greatest motivation for stewarding our bodies well.

We might experience various hindrances to activity throughout our lives—maybe through a disability, chronic health issue, pregnancy, or other circumstance—but we can still uniquely reflect and celebrate God's good design for recreation, even as we await a future of perfect freedom and movement with heavenly bodies one day.

Physical fitness is also a tool God has given us to serve others, offering our bodies as living sacrifices of worship. As we strive to keep our bodies active, we can be the kind of mothers that are quick to jump off the couch to pick up the living room, to play tag in the yard when the neighbor kids ask, to carry in groceries for an elderly neighbor, and to run from point A to point B at our teen's cross-country meet to cheer them on. When our bodies are used to movement, we're more ready to serve when asked, more able to work when needed, and more primed to do the "good works, which God prepared beforehand" (Ephesians 2:10). Even the small act of moving our mouths into a smile can benefit others, showing the welcoming face of a mother whose joy rests in Jesus.

As mothers, there will be seasons where our movement is at a minimum due to circumstances (such as pregnancy, postpartum, or illness) and other seasons where we have the freedom and ability to prioritize more intentional activity. As life and bodies allow, let's be mothers that embrace movement and activity as much as we're physically able. Just as our children grow in their capabilities to crawl, then walk, then run, our joy for recreation can grow right along with theirs. Let's see the wonder of the human body and marvel at how God made us to live and to move.

WHEN YOU CAN'T BE
A PERFECT MOM

EMILY

Too often, I focus on my self-constructed image of the "perfect" mom. Instead of working with the energy the Holy Spirit provides in the work God has put before me, I clench my fists and drag the weight of "not good enough" as I press on to attain my idea of godly motherhood.

I mean, can't we all produce that image we compare ourselves to in a quick second?

A good mom...
has this type of personality
keeps her house in this type of way
does these activities with her children
works this amount
gets up and goes to sleep at these hours
has this type of physical appearance
serves this type of food
engages in this style of hospitality

When we're really supposed to submit to Christ, taking on his easy yoke, responding to his daily direction for the circumstances and family he's given us—we give our hearts over to this specific image of motherhood in our minds.

And one day, we realize we don't have much joy. We're not thriving in our gifts. We're not even focused on the things our husbands really care about. We're obsessed with what our mom friends are doing. We're living anxious that all these days of "not good enough" are adding up to us becoming a big failure.

The Bible doesn't spell out many of the culturally relative details about the way motherhood looks in the practical areas of daily life. Most of the instructions God gives are about our hearts. When we think about what God has actually called us to do and remember that he's already made complete peace with us through the cross, we can cease striving for our perfect idea of motherhood.

We labor to advance the gospel by God's power. We strive to obey the things God has laid out for us to do instead of perfectly keeping rules in areas he hasn't even mentioned in the Bible.

So rest today, Mama—love your husband. Love your kids. Lay down your life. Worship the Lord in all you do.

FOR YOUR POSTPARTUM BODY

LAURA

Culture tells us our bodies should be flawless, unblemished, perfect—even after holding life—but the reality our postpartum bodies shows us is we are everything but.

Sometimes I wonder if we mothers dislike our bodies not for what they are—scarred, shifted, dimpled, and soft—it's that we dislike them for what they are not: godlike.

Culture tells us the solution is to "learn to love our bodies." To find all the things your body can do, and thank it for them. While gratitude can be a good practice, eventually, enough time passes and all of us find that there are days where our bodies don't seem very loveable, no matter how much we have worked to fall in love with them.

Instead, we have to go back to the root: to accept that we are not and were never meant to be divine.

Think of Christ. He wasn't ashamed of his human flesh. Of his marred skin. Of his scarred hands and feet. Jesus used his body to serve and sacrifice, a tool for the overflow of his love for us. His body was like ours. Not what the world says is beautiful but what he says is beautiful.

And so for every stretch mark, for every C-section scar, for the lumps and sags and lines the world tells us we should erase, what if we shut out the shouts of culture and instead follow the model of our Savior? What if instead of seeing our imperfections as repelling, we see what they represent?

The gift of our children from God.

The sacrifice and service of motherhood.

Love marked forever on our bodies.

A sacred connection with our Savior.

Instead of striving to "love" our postpartum bodies, what if we live unashamed of our imperfections?

It's there we stop asking our bodies to be something they are not and never will be. We can make peace with our bodies because Christ made peace with us.

We know who we are: not gods, sitting high on a throne in heaven. We are mothers, sitting on the floor, toys and crumbs all around us, serving the One True God.

WHEN YOU FEEL DISCOURAGED

LAURA

One thing I've found to be true in motherhood is that I will never be perfect. Whether because of natural human limitations or personal sin, there are always areas I can improve. Even on my most excellent mothering days, I can always find a flaw.

But God. His grace covers my days, both the good and bad, and turns my meager offerings into a pleasant aroma for my King. And the thing I know deep in my heart but have such trouble remembering is that's right where God wants me to be. He doesn't want me seeking affirmation from friends, books, or the internet, telling me I have everything to offer and I am enough. Nor does he want me listening to the little voice in my head that tells me I'm awful and will never be enough. Instead, he wants me to remember that only God gets to determine my worth. Because of the work of his Son, I don't have to be perfect; I just have to keep walking in faith each day.

And this is how I continue, even when I feel discouragement from my failures creeping in. In my weakness, God is strong. Ultimately, it's not about feeling shame or pride about what I can or can't do; it's about learning to rest in his love and grace knowing that each time I come to the end of myself, I can find a life-giving new beginning in him.

FOR IF YOU'VE HAD
A TRAUMATIC BIRTH

LAURA

In the moments between my body beginning contractions and finally meeting my firstborn, I came the closest to mortality I had ever been. As I replayed my child's birth in my mind, I couldn't help but wonder, "Did it have to go that way? Did we make the right choices? Could there have been an easier way?" I struggled to process all that happened or even know *how* to think about it. But eventually, when I was pregnant with my second child and sitting in my midwife's office, I broke down in tears telling the midwife how scared I was of childbirth. When I was finished, she handed me a tissue and said, "Oh honey, you had a traumatic birth."

In a fallen world, our culture tells us to worship the female body, that it was built to give birth and it should be the most natural thing in the world. But the curse on Eve and childbearing is a reality all women live with. It is no longer natural; it's unnatural, pocketed with imperfection, speckled with sin. All of today's natural childbirth books in the world can tell us that we women are "warriors," and with the right mental outlook, "birth can be a wonderful, pain-free experience." And while I don't doubt that some stories of a joy-filled, natural labor and delivery are true (because we serve a God who is lavish with his grace, even in a sinful world), for most of us, our experiences with giving birth miss the mark in some way.

But there is hope. Coming to us through the very same process we struggle through, the very process made painful: Mary carried Christ for nine months, laboring, groaning, and finally delivering our Redeemer in a barn. It was through childbirth that God sent our Redeemer, who would eventually bear the curse on the cross, taking our pain and replacing it with hope.

And it's here that we work through a difficult or traumatic birth. We first put our suffering in its rightful place: remembering that imperfect births are a reality of the Fall, bringing with it imperfect providers, decisions, medications, and advocacy. But these are the things God uses to draw us to himself. The outward groaning of us in childbirth points to creation's inward groaning for the coming of the true King. As we long for redemption from the pains of childbirth, our hearts long for the true redemption that will come with the return of our Savior.

And it's through this lens we can process a traumatic or difficult birth story. Here are some things that can help you take those redemptive steps.

Take time to mourn your experience. Healing happens when we bring things into the light. Acknowledge your feelings with your husband, a trusted friend, maybe even a professional.

Remind yourself that God is sovereign over all that happened at your child's birth. All things are created and done to glorify him. Even if it didn't go according to your plan, God is still good. Do you love him more than your "perfect" plan?

Find the grace. God's grace is everywhere! Imperfect births are part of the Fall, but there are many areas that God still grants us grace that we don't deserve. Doctors, doulas, monitors, medications, air conditioners, comfortable beds, birthing tubs, the fact that our husbands can be by our sides during childbirth—the graces are endless when you start thinking through them.

Forgive your providers for areas you've been wronged. Release the bitterness and anger at the base of the cross. Remember that they are also human and make mistakes. Because you've been forgiven, you can forgive the wrongs done against you.

Remember your true identity. You are not a "goddess"; you are human. Don't worship the created instead of the Creator. If you feel ashamed that you "couldn't do it" or you were not "woman enough," remind yourself that you are limited. God is the giver of life, and it's Christ's perfect sacrifice on the cross that bridges the chasm between our bodies and the ability to be a life-giver.

See your birth experience as a way to point others to Christ. In your weakness, he is strong. Find ways to highlight his goodness in your birth story. Remember a difficult birth is not your final story, but only a shadow of your true life to come. Birth and its pain, imperfections, and unknowns are things that point to our need for a Savior who will one day come and deliver us.

For me, the process of healing came slowly. But once it was unearthed, I was surprised to find how God transformed it from something scary and hard to something filled with meaning, grace, and love, pointing me to redemption and gratefulness for all that Christ has done.

FOR WHEN YOU
ARE ANGRY

———————

Don't believe the lie that you're stuck where you are. Though there are some things you might not be able to change, you are not defined by your personality, sinful tendencies, or current skill set. You are a new creation in Christ, and because of God, you can change, grow, and improve in faithfulness to the things God loves and cares about. Trust that God is bigger than anything you face. He is making all things new, even you.

LAURA

FOR THE WORST
PARTS OF US

LAURA

Sometimes, parenting feels like a gut punch. When we think about our children's behavior and how to help, we're often left with feelings of uncertainty, fear, and insufficiency—we see their sin and have no idea what to do.

And then we see our own sin revealed as we deal with theirs. It's exhausting. And if you quickly fall into despair, you're not alone.

But there is hope!

Because the amazing truth is, God is bigger than your child's sin. He is bigger than *your* sin. He is bigger than your failed attempts, your inadequate abilities, your tendency to overreact, or your desire to be lazy. None of us can keep God's law perfectly, not our children and not ourselves. But you know what? Christ gave himself up on the cross in our place so instead, we can be lifted and enveloped by his beautiful, perfect, holy mercy and grace.

None of us are good, but that just means we can rejoice all the more with our children in Christ's sacrifice on the cross. Nothing is beyond the reach of his grace. His redemption can heal even the worst parts of us.

This is the message your children need to hear. This is the message you need to hear. It is the only thing that will bring true comfort to our hearts.

Preach this truth to yourself, every day: God is bigger than your sin, and he is bigger than your child's sin. He does the saving, not you.

This is a great hope indeed.

BECAUSE IT'S USUALLY UNREALISTIC EXPECTATIONS

EMILY

When I consider a common source of my irritability, it often comes back to one word: expectations.

I expect my children to act like little adults. I expect them to make me look like I'm doing a wonderful job. I expect them not to overreact or ignore my direction. I expect to always hold it together, finding ways to strategically organize my life so I can magically do more. I expect to have the life I want without having to put forth too much effort.

And in these expectations of myself and others, the stage is set for disappointment—for anger, frustration, grief, irritability.

Part of applying the gospel to my hard-to-please heart is admitting that my expectations aren't always realistic or rooted in truth.

While it's a real and necessary part of life to set expectations for those around me, I lose sight of the big picture when I forget that my greatest expectations and hopes can only be met in Jesus. Everyone else will fail and fall short in one way or another.

Resting in him brings such freedom! Not only from my sinful tendencies, but from my unrealistic expectations. Knowing that all God's expectations for me were fully met in Jesus means that I don't have to shame myself (or others) when my expectations go unmet. I can turn my eyes back to him and rest in grace.

WHEN YOU ARE ANNOYED

EMILY

Motherhood provides plenty of opportunities for sound effects. Sighing when a child knocks on the bathroom door. Huffing when a little helper drips dishrag water across the newly mopped floor. Letting out a guttural "grrr" when the children erupt into another argument. Shrieking when the toddler gets too close to the edge. While many of these are understandable (and some warranted), I'm learning that humility doesn't leave room for grumbling (Philippians 2:14-18).

When I respond to unwanted circumstances or interruptions with a grumble, deep down, what I often mean is,

"I shouldn't have to take care of you right now."

"You're taking from *my* time."

"I'm tired of serving."

These feelings and statements are a lot to unpack—too much for this short reflection. God has designed us to need regular patterns of rest, and we should use wisdom as we pour out to others. We're not meant to go it alone, and sometimes, groans help us identify places where we need more support.

But what the Lord is showing me is that in many cases, the narratives that repeat in my mind until they erupt in a sound effect are a result of my pride. Pride says that I am in charge of my own life. That I have a right to do whatever I want, when I want, on the terms I want. Pride says that I should be served, not serve. Pride says I don't need God.

The big punch to my pride is a long look at the Savior. I'm glad Jesus didn't huff and grumble at my needs—instead, he willingly came to save and serve. He willingly obeyed the Father. He met needs, let others seemingly interrupt, took the form of a servant, and gave the ultimate sacrifice—his very life so that others would live. He didn't count equality with God as a thing to be grasped, but humbled himself.

As I walk through my day, I pray God fills my heart with this truth, because it transforms interruptions into opportunities to worship and glorify God. I'm praying that my grumbles turn into great praises and that my huffs turn into heartfelt thanksgiving.

Let's make a joyful noise to the Lord. We serve others because he served.

WHEN YOU ARE INTERRUPTED

LAURA

In motherhood, interruptions are frequent. Whether it's a child getting out of bed four times to ask for a drink of water when you've just sat down to relax, or a late-night talk with a teen about things going on at school when you really need to prepare for work the next day—interruptions are a regular part of motherhood.

How do you respond when you're interrupted? What do you do when your heart was set on one plan, but it's clear those you care for need something else? Are you kind? Or frustrated? Are you patient? Or bothered?

They say interruptions reveal who we truly are, and it's easy to be irritated by them. But what would happen if we started to see the interruptions in our day as from the Lord? What if we scheduled less and paused more, asking the Spirit what he might have for us? What if we made room in our day specifically to be interrupted?

If we look carefully, we'll see that God uses the inconveniences and disruptions from our children to shape and form us not just as mothers but as women of God. In each interruption, we have the opportunity to choose: Will we say, not just with our mouths but with our actions, "Yes, Lord, I will trust you with my time, my money, my words, my comforts, my desires?"

It is these moments of interruption that often reveal the true heart behind our ministry in motherhood.

Today, let's pray for sanctified sight to see the needs in our homes through the eyes of Christ. Let's walk in holiness and obedience with ears that hear the Spirit say, "This is the way, walk in it" (Isaiah 30:21).

WHEN YOU ARE FRUSTRATED

_____

LAURA

When I find myself feeling frustrated with my children more often than normal, it can be easy for me to spiral downward, feeling guilt and condemnation and listening to the lie that I cannot change.

But when I believe this lie, what's really happening is I'm believing that I am beyond the reach of God's grace—I'm believing that the cross wasn't enough.

I can honestly say there has never been a time in my life that I have seen the gospel more clearly than when I became a mom and started to see my unrighteous anger, impatience, and irritability come to the surface.

The sin, hidden beneath for so many years, rose in full strength to the surface in motherhood. But God can change me. It is the dim backdrop of my sin that allows the gospel to shine bright. Because God's grace is magnified when we rest in his power and trust his work on the cross to be sufficient.

May we be like Paul, who was able to "boast all the more gladly of my weakness, so that the power of Christ may rest upon me" (2 Corinthians 12:9).

Don't give up on fighting your sin, Mom. Be obedient, and fight in the power of the Spirit, knowing the shock over your own sin is a chance for you to grow deeper in relationship with your Father. Rejoice in your weakness because it is a mercy that shows your desperate need for God's grace through Christ.

BECAUSE TODAY IS A NEW DAY

EMILY

You don't have to be defined by what you did yesterday.

Yes, there are hard days. There are days when your weakness and inability seem to be the only things on display for your family and the world. There are days when you feel more needy than helpful and more sinful than holy. There are days when you are in disbelief, wondering, "How is God using me in the midst of my lack?"

Maybe yesterday felt like that (or maybe your whole week felt that way).

I'm not saying that it's all okay, but...it's not the end of the story! Just as God shed blood after the sin in the garden to provide a covering for Adam and Eve, just like God had the Israelites slaughter the lamb to cover their doorposts with blood so that death would pass them over, just like God redeemed Ruth by grafting her into the family of God, he overcomes your sin and he covers it with the blood of Christ, bringing you into a new family of faith.

And if you have faith in what Christ did for you on the cross, then you can move on from what happened yesterday. Not in an "Oh I'll just ignore that and sweep it under the rug" kind of way, but with a heart at peace, knowing nothing can separate you from the love of God in Christ Jesus.

Wait—did you hear that? *Nothing* can separate you from God's love if you are *in him*.

Not what you did on Saturday, not what you did on Sunday, and not what you did yesterday. So lay your brokenness at the cross, see what it cost, be sad, rejoice, and press on today with your eyes fixed on the blessed Redeemer.

BECAUSE JOY OVERFLOWS

EMILY

Have you ever been around someone who has unexplainable joy? Did you walk away from your time with them wanting a bit of that yourself? Feeling lighter or more drawn to Christ? This is what it feels like when joy spreads. When we find our joy in Christ, we get filled up, and it overflows into relationships, decisions, and actions. We can bring sincere and lasting encouragement to others—pointing them to the true source of hope.

WHEN YOU FEEL LIKE
TWO DIFFERENT MOMS

LAURA

I am the fun, happy, bright, and engaged mom. The one that dances in the kitchen, builds elaborate train tracks that run through the hallway into the living room, and tosses her toddlers over and over again in the air until her arms shake.

I am the frustrated, discontented, lazy mom. The one that rushes through bedtime feeling like she might scream if she has to read another book, turns up the music so she can't hear the whining in the backseat, and expects her children to stop sinning even though she hasn't.

I live in the in-between. Feeling like I might split in two. Must I always be both? She is so flawed, inconsistent, imperfect.

And it is here, in the crack that spreads down the middle, I find who I truly am: I am the mother that revels in the in-between. One mom shows me I am a sinner in need of a Savior; the other mom reveals the grace I've been given by my Savior.

I am both, I am two, I am she.

WHEN YOU FEEL LIKE
THE DAY IS LOST

LAURA

The day is never too far gone, too far lost—it's never a day so terrible that you can't recover and your only option is to give up. All things can be redeemed. Even your attitude.

So what do we do? We readjust our hearts to stop focusing on the negative and, instead, repeat truth and repent. (It's called "preaching the gospel to yourself.") We confess our failures, we ask forgiveness, and we turn away from our sin and toward Jesus.

We choose joy. We choose love. We choose peace, patience, kindness, goodness, faithfulness, gentleness, and self-control. We choose Christ.

Don't think of it as pulling yourself up by your bootstraps because you're definitely not doing that. What you're doing when you choose to redeem your attitude is living out the redemption story of the grace of God and the sacrifice of his Son. Because of Christ, we don't have to be stuck in a cycle of "bad mom." Instead, we can rest in our identity in him and allow Christ to be strong where we are weak.

Mom, you can change your attitude because of how he changed your life.

WHEN YOU NEED JOY

EMILY

Is joy the feeling we get when someone brings us our favorite latte? Is it the sensation of cradling a clean, snuggly baby in our arms? The loving connection in a healthy marriage?

Merriam-Webster says that joy is the "experience of great pleasure and delight," so many of those examples qualify. Taken broadly, joy is available in life's ideal moments—when we're laughing with our kids or dipping our toes into the ocean. But is this what the Bible means when it refers to joy, especially as a fruit of the Holy Spirit working in our hearts?

The Greek word for joy in Galatians is *chara*. I'm no Greek scholar, but a review of other verses in the Bible that use that word gives us a better picture. We see the word *chara* used to explain the joy of Christ's birth announcement, a Christian's experience of coming into the presence of God after being found faithful, a gift that Christ gives his disciples, and the response of seeing the gospel spread. It's a word that describes God's kingdom and the result of a unified church. But before we think that it's only rainbows and butterflies, it's also a word present in affliction. The Bible tells us that Jesus endured the cross because of "the joy that was set before him" (Hebrews 12:2), and that joy can be present in deep suffering.

Here's some good news for moms who have never experienced their ideal day or who feel like nothing goes right—joy is found in a person, not a set of circumstances.

Who could possibly be this perfect, steadfast, everlasting, and powerful? Who could be such a source of warm feelings in our soul on good days and hard ones? Jesus Christ.

One of my favorite verses talks about this source. In it, the psalmist says, "You make known to me the path of life; in your presence there is fullness of joy; at your right hand are pleasures forevermore" (Psalm 16:11). When I used to read this, I imagined an ambiguous orb of glowing light at God's right hand. Or maybe some scenes of heaven—flowering fields and smiling saints. But the verse took on a completely new meaning when I realized who is sitting there—Jesus Christ.

If we want to know joy, we must know Jesus. To know Jesus, we have to stop finding joy in lesser things, even our ideal version of motherhood. We have to believe that Jesus is alive and seated at the right hand of God, and follow him all the days of our lives. We have to walk with him—reading the Scriptures, spending time in prayer, and meditating on who he is and what he's done.

BECAUSE WE ALL
SPREAD SOMETHING

EMILY

As moms, we see how excitement spreads. Phrases like "Cookies are ready!" or "Movie time!" suddenly propel kids to skip stairs on the way up from the basement or bound in from the backyard (tromping mud) right to our side. We're also aware of the way laughter spreads when someone accidentally shoots milk out of their nose or makes a silly sound from a body part. Once the giggles start, it's over. And sadly, moms are also familiar with the spread of pain through bickering, bullying, or bad words that lead to tears and broken relationships.

Spreading isn't just something we do to things (like peanut butter on toast); it's a thing that happens to us and through us. Spreading is what it sounds like—taking something that was once concentrated and pushing the boundaries outward until more area is covered. More toast coated. More people roped in. What we spread matters.

At the beginning of the Bible, God spread his light, life, glory, and goodness throughout the world he created. Mankind was blessed as they received from his hand. But then the serpent entered and spread darkness, doubt, and lies. And soon after, Romans 5:12 tells us, "death spread to all men." Adam's sin meant death for all. The creation story helps us understand why it's so natural for mankind to spread evil in the world, though we were made to spread the glory of God throughout creation.

But when Jesus came to earth, died, rose from the grave, and ascended, he came to spread life. Jesus stopped death by washing and cleansing us with his blood. With a new heart, now our lives and words can be the aroma of Christ to others.

This might feel a little heady for someone just trying to get breakfast on the table before the toddler has a meltdown, but stick with me—have you ever considered what you spread to those around you? What will it be today? I hope it's him.

FOR WHEN YOU ARE ONLINE

God knows us better than anyone else,
and he sees more than our filtered photos
and cute selfies. He sees us when we look
like a hot mess and when our hearts are
a hot mess, and he loves us anyway.
It's really God who we ultimately need
to look to for affirmation and that
deep sense of being known and loved.

EMILY

WHEN YOU ARE ON
SOCIAL MEDIA

LAURA

Sometimes, I think to myself, "I feel overwhelmed in life and motherhood; I'm gonna hop on IG because I don't know how else to handle it." It's not conscious, but it's the reality of what's happening.

I have to wonder, though, *am I overwhelmed because of my motherhood, and so I run to Instagram? Or am I overwhelmed because of Instagram, so I run from my motherhood?*

I don't think there's always a clear-cut answer. But more and more, I'm realizing that it's probably the latter. The effects are barely perceptible— because social media is addictive and we're idol-making factories and all that. Yet, where I was content before, I'm now unhappy. Where I was confident before, I'm now second-guessing. Where I was at peace, I'm now wringing my hands and texting my husband, "*Did you see this?*"

If you're like me, you usually think of social media as harmless. That the

benefits outweigh the negatives. That you're strong enough not to be pulled under. But that's sort of like eating a bunch of donuts for lunch, then thinking you'll never experience a sugar crash. It doesn't mean we can't ever enjoy a donut; it simply means we have to be wise and realistic about its impact.

Maybe it's not that we have no friends or giftings or accomplishments or that our lives are not good ones—it's that we've allowed social media to creep and claw its way to the top of the throne of our hearts.

Moms, we have to wake up to the realities of social media. It's not that we can't be on it, but we have to understand its effects. And perhaps in doing that, we'll find we run to God when we're overwhelmed rather than social media.

And maybe, just maybe, with Christ steadfast on the throne of our hearts, we'll know the right place to go when we feel overwhelmed.

WHEN YOU FORGET
THEY ARE REAL PEOPLE

_____

EMILY AND LAURA

We're millennials, so we remember the thrill of joining Facebook soon after it launched. The network was only open to college students at the time, and we each anticipated the coveted .edu email address needed to create a profile. Immediately, we began posting pictures, tagging friends in posts, and sharing about our days.

Social media was the Wild West of the online world, and no one was quite sure how to act. There were no blog posts about online etiquette. No podcasts about how to best execute an Instagram presence. No warnings about social media consumption and mental health.

Today, we know that social media has pitfalls. It can be helpful; it can be terrible. While social media isn't right for everyone, if you are using it, perhaps you're like us, confronting the same choice each time you open the apps: Will you use social media as an opportunity to honor God and love others, or to serve yourself and your own agenda?

In many instances, these waters feel murky. *Am I sharing this photo of my kids for quick likes or am I weighing the costs of their online image? Is sharing a picture of my kids mostly about me wanting attention or about letting extended family see what we're up to? Is telling people about my small business self-serving or God-honoring? Is sharing about my faith a way to glorify God or to draw attention to my own righteousness? Is commenting and liking an opportunity to build gospel relationships or a means to expand my network?* And the answer is likely both. Because like anything in the Christian life, where does one motive end and the other begin?

Just as social media can be a tool to advance the gospel or spread the word about something we steward, it can also be used to leverage people for our own aims. Have you ever heard the question, "Will I love people, or will I leverage people?" It's a good (and convicting) diagnostic for many situations. Whether you use social media casually to show photos of your growing family, share lifestyle hacks, post on behalf of your employer, or market your small business, we all should grapple with how our faith in Christ shapes our social media use.

At its essence, leveraging people puts pressure on them to do or be something for our benefit. While Scripture exhorts us to freely serve others, leveraging looks for ways for others to serve us. We may have good intentions—our cause may be worthy and our message important—but Christians should pause before adopting a leveraging mindset.

Leveraging can lead to writing clickbait titles, embellishing the truth, intentionally preying on people's felt needs, or using photographic misrepresentation. It can lead us to view those in our own home as content sources to be posed for pictures or filmed for our ideal montage. When leveraging is our mindset, we're quick to ask how followers or influencers can meet our desires—giving us instant feedback, answers to our questions, emotional support, and affirmation. In these moments, we're primarily concerned with how others can serve our agenda instead of humbly thinking about how we all might serve the Lord's.

But God's image-bearers are not a resource to be consumed—they're human beings to value and serve. Social media can be a place where we share "whatever is true, whatever is honorable, whatever is just, whatever is pure, whatever is lovely, whatever is commendable" (Philippians 4:8). And this isn't so we can grow our platforms and gain more likes; our place on social media is ground to be given in service to the King.

Loving others on social media means we refrain from thinking of followers as "fans" or influencers as vending machines and instead picture individual persons who need the grace of Christ. It means prayerfully considering the role our children, family, and home should play in our content online and taking care to protect their dignity. A loving mindset remembers that real people are affected by the things we share, say, and post. Our posts can induce things like joy, tears, confession, or reconciliation. They can even tempt people to sin. While we can't control the way each post is received, Christian love seeks to post and comment on content that's genuinely helpful, truthful, and God-glorifying.

As Christian moms on social media, our aim is not to be Instagram worthy but to share about Christ's infinite worth. This won't mean communicating about Jesus in every post, but it will mean patterning our lives after him in all we say and do.

WHEN YOU NEED DISCERNMENT

EMILY

Shopping for peaches is surprisingly challenging. As you survey the bin of fruit, you'll notice a wide array of options. Some will be shriveled and rotten looking. Some will look good overall, with a few bruises that you'll have to cut off. Some will be near-perfect, and you'll eagerly drop them into your bag. And some will look awesome, but when you get them home and dig in, they will be brown and flavorless inside.

While this experience rings true at the grocery store, it also somewhat rings true as we pick through Christian resources for motherhood. Some books, blogs, and articles are obviously not true or healthy. Many are going to be a mixture—helpful truths that apply in some situations alongside other things that aren't helpful or true for every mom. Some are going to be wonderful (but not perfect), and you'll pass those around to your friends as trusted resources. And unfortunately, some will come highly recommended, but once you read them, you discover they aren't helpful at all.

It's good to remember these things as we sift through the "peach bin" of resources for motherhood. We can spur one another on toward godliness and good works in Christ as we become literate in biblical truth and have great conversations about how those truths apply to our lives.

Don't avoid shopping for peaches just because you might get a dud—do your best to discern truth, live in community with other women who can help you figure it out, and never stop growing in your own knowledge of God's Word.

WHEN YOU DON'T UNDERSTAND ANOTHER MOM

EMILY

Differences with other moms can surprise us at every turn, even in the most common situations. When we see a mom at the park feeding her kids a bento box of apple slices, nuts, and cheese while we dig an old container of cereal out from the bottom of our bag, we insecurely notice that one of us spends much more time on food prep. When we go to the library armed with a predetermined list of educational literature, while another mom's kids seem to grab anything that looks cool off the shelves, we can't comprehend how she lets them do that.

It's challenging to know how to make peace with our differences—in culture, food preferences, activity levels, family sizes, and more. But we can always recount our similarities. We moms are all made in the image of God. And as Christian moms, we all were once far off and hostile to God, but through the sacrifice of his own Son, he tore down the dividing wall of hostility and brought us to himself. He took the first step, he loved us while we were still sinners, and he teaches us to be more like him.

What does this mean for our interaction with the believing mom who is different from us? With a heart that is humbled by God's reconciliation with us through Christ—fully knowing we don't have it all together and we haven't cornered the market on "good" motherhood—we can bear with her in love. We can be gentle and patient with that other mom, as we want her to be patient with us. We can seek to understand the unique challenges that she faces and the choices that she makes in an effort to obey God and raise her children in the Lord.

Instead of making snap judgments, sizing other moms up, and making broad brushstroke statements about "moms who work" or "moms who stay at home" or "moms who homeschool" and so on, let's seek to be kind and generous with our assumptions. Let's resolve to learn the Scriptures together with our sisters and pursue Christ, living out the gospel in our daily lives. Let's lovingly help one another see and understand different perspectives in matters of conscience.

Peace with the different mom but sister-in-Christ is possible. It comes through the cross as a subsequent overflow from peace in our vertical relationship with God. Unity is going to come not from everyone-is-like-me motherhood but from every-believer-made-one-in-him theology.

BECAUSE WE ALL NEED
WISDOM ONLINE

EMILY

Moms are good at spotting danger. Our eyes scan every environment for risks because we're deeply concerned about keeping our kids safe. When we see risks, almost subconsciously, we take action—if it's a busy street, we grab a little hand and give stern instruction to stay close. If it's a high tower on the playground, we stand below, reminding our child to hold on and not lean over the edge. When it comes to keeping our kids safe, we're quick to establish and enforce boundaries.

But when it comes to our own social media use and the ambiguous danger of life online, how many of us act like our children, running free without concern for risks? How many of us scroll with no boundaries, forgetting that there might be "busy streets" and "high towers" where the dangers aren't physical but mental, emotional, relational, and spiritual?

Proverbs 22:3 gives some wisdom we could use for social media today: "The prudent sees danger and hides himself, but the simple go on and suffer for it." Said another way, this has modern application: A prudent woman sees the potential dangers of social media and takes protective measures, but a foolish woman just scrolls endlessly without boundaries and suffers for it.

Just like every child is at risk for different things and needs their own parents to assess dangers and set boundaries, we all have different personalities and are susceptible to different risks online. Some of us might be easily swayed by influencers, while others are easily enticed by the latest controversy. Some of us might be lulled into mindless lurking, while others might feel the pull to post every moment of our day.

Whatever the danger may be, each of us can learn to assess the risks of social media in our own lives with our own sinful tendencies and then apply the Word of God. We can "hide ourselves" in the Lord, turning to him for wisdom, guidance, and protection.

As moms who are good at spotting danger, let's not forget to look for it in our own daily social media habits. Let's press pause and see where God might have us take precautions.

WHEN YOU DON'T KNOW
WHO TO LISTEN TO

EMILY

There's a lot of pressure on moms these days. From social media to culture to our own friend groups, we're left wondering which path is best. Who do I obey? How do I obey? What do I obey? We might be able to keep up with the pressures of motherhood for a little while on our own, but eventually, we will come to the end of our rope. We will find that we can't ever do enough.

In our decisions and moments of weakness, we will all turn to something. We all obey something—or someone. And if we're followers of Jesus, obedience to him comes first.

Obedience to Christ lifts the pressure because he met the standard of perfection on our behalf—being the once-and-for-all sacrifice for sin. We no longer live in a constant state of fear that we'll never measure up. Instead, we live in a constant state of submission to him. We know we're moms who could never do enough but who follow a Savior who did.

In light of this, God's commands aren't burdensome. They're freeing. They give life. They're chances for us to show our gratitude and worship. They're paths to joy and flourishing in motherhood, even if our circumstances aren't always "good" by the world's definition.

Obedience to Christ might not tell us whether or not to sign our daughter up for ballet, but it will make us consider eternal things as we make the decision. It might not tell us exactly which house to buy, but it will give us the perspective to use our home as a place of peace and hospitality. The questions we have about if we're doing enough as moms find their answers in Jesus.

Jesus says, "If you love me, you will keep my commandments" (John 14:15). And if we love Jesus, he says we can keep his commands because he's given us his Spirit and his righteousness.

FOR KINGDOM SUCCESS

LAURA

In the kingdom economy, success isn't measured by dollars and cents, awards and compliments, or followers and influence. Success is a life sold out for Christ, which pursues God's glory, not our own. Yes, God is concerned with what we do. But more than what we do—in the bounds of his commands—he's concerned with how we do it.

FOR THE COMPARISON GAME

LAURA

For me, it usually starts with the mom that's super crafty. You know, the ones that create daily activities with baking soda, construction paper, and old soup cans to teach their three-year-old science, art, and generally how to have an imagination?

I throw soup cans in the recycling bin without a second thought.

Somewhere, deep down, I want to be like that mom. If I'm honest, it's because I'm afraid if I'm not, my kids will be behind their peers in school, or they'll have "boring" memories from childhood. Or the biggest one: I fear someone will say I'm not a good enough mom.

Do you have anything like that? An area in your life you compare yourself to another mom? Maybe it's your home and decor, or your meals and snacks, or your body image and workout routine, or even another mom's ability to parent her children with her seemingly endless well of patience and self-control.

The options are endless when it comes to comparison.

But the beautiful thing about the gospel is we're free from feeling like a failure because other moms are not our measuring stick. You don't need to image another woman because you are called to image Christ. The moment he was crushed on the cross was the moment you became free from the crushing weight of comparison.

God intentionally created you with unique talents and giftings specifically for the children he gave you to mother. In him, you aren't defined by your skills—cooking/decorating/crafting/working/parenting—you're defined by Christ's sacrificial work on the cross. Which means you have complete freedom to live out the mom God created you to be—not the mom you feel like you should be.

Which means it's okay to throw the soup cans in the recycling bin if you want.

God doesn't desire you to strive to be like another mother; he desires you to strive to be like Christ.

Today, let go of the fear that you won't be enough as a mother if you don't do that "thing" you feel you are lacking in. Because of Christ's death and resurrection, you are enough, exactly the way you are.

FOR WHEN IT'S HARD TO FOLLOW GOD

At some point you have to ask, Is Jesus most glorious to you? Do you love God the most? Are you in awe of him? Because if God is not on the throne in your heart, then why would you pray? You're not going to see him as powerful enough to make any changes in your life.

LAURA

WHEN YOU DON'T HAVE TIME TO PRAY

LAURA

Susanna Wesley had eleven children and still found time to pray.

You may have never heard of her, but you may have heard of two of her sons: John and Charles Wesley, two men who impacted millions of lives for Jesus. Amid the noise and activity of her many children, Susanna's trick was to pull her apron over her head—signaling to them and anyone else around that she was in prayer and not to be disturbed.

We live in an age when moms consistently lament not being able to go to the bathroom alone, yet Susanna found a way to have time alone by disappearing under a piece of fabric. Like a giant "Do Not Disturb" sign, her children knew Momma was to be left alone as she brought her prayers and requests to God in the middle of the noise and bustle a full household brings.

I can't tell you how many times I've heard from other women that they wish their "prayer life was better." And while the phrase can sound trite, it's true for most of us—myself included. Over the years, I've tried a lot of different things to grow in the area of prayer. I've studied it in God's Word, read what others say about it, asked for tips from friends, purchased tools, made special plans, and so on. And while plans and tools are great, often as a mom, I don't always have the luxury of sitting with thirty minutes of quiet to write down my prayers. As a mother, life is typically loud, messy, and ever-changing, and it's easy to quickly stop being consistent in my prayer life if that's what I rely on.

When it comes to prayer, we don't need to overcomplicate it or make it more intense or scary than it is. Prayer is simply talking with God. This means the key to prayer is *simply praying.*

Prayer is a gift from our Heavenly Father, something we are never too busy for and it is never too noisy for. Even though I'm willing to bet most of us don't don an apron all that often, what if we all took a page from Susanna's book? It's good news for all of us moms that we can pray any time, any place, about anything, asking for God's power to work in our lives.

Here are a few ways you can incorporate Susanna's apron in your life.

Quiet your heart, even if everything else is loud. Start here. As moms, finding time and quiet is an elusive combination. So while you may not be able to find these two things together, take time as often as you can to focus on your Redeemer and all you have access to because of Christ's death on the cross and resurrection from the grave. Remember your eternal security, and ask God to bring your will in line with his. A friend of mine always says, "Our position in Christ will determine our posture in prayer." Trust that God will show up and he will fulfill his promises in your life. Pray as a loved child, not an orphan.

Act on the urge to pray. How many times a day do we feel a need to pray, but don't do it? When we lose our keys, when we are in the midst of a particularly difficult discipline moment, as we talk with a friend who is struggling—the prompting we feel to pray is from the Holy Spirit. Don't resist him. To have your heart moved and your mind prompted to pray is a gift. Thank God for it. Act on the impulse, and you'll be surprised how much more time you'll spend in prayer each day.

Bring every little thing to God. In the kingdom economy, there is no "small thing." Remember, God cares about the sparrow, the hairs on our head, the bread that we eat, and the shirt that we wear. Nothing is outside of God's control and will for our lives, so no matter how minute or mundane, remember that the God in heaven cares about it.

Give it time. Sometimes, it's a quick one-word cry like "Help!" as we see our toddler throw themselves on the floor in a tantrum and we have no idea what to do. Other times, we may find twenty minutes while the kids are in a piano lesson. A healthy prayer life includes both long and short times of prayer. We need God every moment, so don't forget him in the tiniest moments, but also don't neglect to give him larger chunks of your day when you can find it.

Pray with your children. As mothers, our children are with us a lot, which means there are ample opportunities to not just pray for needs *in front of* our children but also pray *with* our children. While this can be before meals and bedtime prayers, I also find repentance to be a key area. While I want to strive to magnify God in all that I say and do around my children, I am an imperfect image-bearer of Christ—which means I should be the chief repenter in my home. Confessing my (appropriate) sins in front of and with my children is the best way I can show them my need for the good news. Not being afraid to engage in prayer with my children not only gives me a chance to pull out my apron more often, but it also teaches them what a life dependent on Christ looks like in the day-to-day.

While our aprons may not be physical pieces of fabric with eyelet trim, we have everything we need each day to throw Susanna's apron over our heads and come to the Lord in prayer.

WHEN YOU NEED A
FRESH WAY TO PRAY

EMILY

It's easy for me to get distracted during prayer. When I pray aloud, my sentences tend to dwindle off as I remember a random task I didn't complete. When I pray in my head, I get stuck on the same phrase or just utter a quick "Amen" because I'm not sure what to pray next.

Every person's learning style and personality are different, so it's good to find different ways to pray. It's why I've adopted different strategies over the years, including reading guided prayers from others and writing my own. If these options feel foreign to you, here are some benefits and a few tips for getting started.

Read the prayers of others when...your mind is blank, because the rich, historical, biblically based prayers can give you words where you have none. This is a great option for moms who aren't sure what to pray or need some fresh ideas and guidance. It's also good for moms who are tired, experiencing brain fog, or going through a season of grief.

Get started: Snag a reliable book of prayers, and keep it with your quiet-time materials. Or just use the Psalms! Set aside three to five minutes to read and pray a prayer every day. Don't just read it to yourself—think about your own life as you pray the Word. You can also add your own thoughts at the end if you have new or different things to pray about after reading.

Write your prayers when...you want to keep your thoughts organized and create a record for you to come back to days, months, or years later. It's an amazing, tangible, and praise-filled way to see God's work and provision! Bonus: Maybe your kids or grandkids can read these someday. This is a great option for moms who already enjoy journaling and wish they had more time to process through writing or for moms who enjoy saving memories and want to see the specific ways God answers their prayers.

Get started: Choose a Bible verse or passage to guide your prayer, find a notebook, and write away. If you aren't sure where to start, write praises and thanksgiving to God, then ask him for what you need. (Quick tip: Consider using discretion with names and details if someone else could read it.)

Don't give up—prayer is always worth it.

WHEN PRAYER CHANGES YOU

LAURA

It was a year or two into motherhood when I realized that in prayer, I didn't actually know what needed to change. Take, for example, a prayer for patience—that I would be kind and wise and slow to speak during the tantrums and incessant requests for snacks. But while my prayer sounded holy, what I really wanted was for my kids to change. To stop interrupting me with any unnecessary needs. I didn't really want patience in hard circumstances; I wanted circumstances that made patience easy.

Yet when a mother asks for the things God loves, like patience, he's going to change her, whether she fully understands what she's asking for or not. To do so, he's going to put things in her path to allow her to practice those elusive fruits of the Spirit as she leans on the Holy Spirit.

That's because prayer is like finally getting out that step stool to get a bird's-eye view of your bookshelves and realizing the staggering depth of dust that really exists there.

Prayer shows us just how much we're trying to build our own kingdom instead of God's.

Right prayer submits who we are—our personality, circumstances, relationships, sufferings, talents, and giftings—to growing in holiness to be like Christ. Admittedly, this is messy, radical, refining work. And those are frightening words, written all in a row. But if we trust God and know he's good, we don't have to be scared.

As you grow in your understanding of God's holiness, the more you will fall in love with God, the more holy you yourself will become, and the more you will treat God as holy as he is. As this happens, the more you will want to worship God, the more you will want to yield to God, and the more you will see and realize God's goodness and grace in all things.

Prayer walks you right into the heart of God and shows you the depths of your sin and all the ways it is outmatched by the depth of God's love.

And when you see that, you cannot leave unchanged.

WHEN THERE IS NO PERFECT TIME TO MEET WITH GOD

LAURA

When it comes to quiet time with God, I often want the ideal.

I want the whole house to be silent so I can have a long string of uninterrupted thoughts. I want my coffee fresh and hot. I want to sit in my favorite chair with a snuggly blanket. I want my journal with a special pen and a well-marked Bible. I tend to think that if all these criteria are met, only *then* will I have a full and fruitful relationship with God.

But that's rarely how it looks. Instead, I'm creeping through a dark house with good intentions, only to groan with frustration when I wake up a child. I'm sipping coffee that's grown cold and trying not to let my journal become too smeared with syrup from breakfast. I'm getting up from my reading again and again to break up a conflict or change a diaper. And because my "ideal" wasn't met, I leave feeling like maybe my time with God didn't count.

However, by God's grace and the wisdom of others, I'm learning my "ideal quiet time" isn't the foundation of my faith. Times of solitude with God are as important as date nights in marriage—it's wonderful and special to sneak away with your husband every so often, but if you're waiting for date night to have a connection with your husband, you probably won't have a thriving relationship.

In the same way, I'm recognizing that my relationship with God is about worshipping him at all times of the day, finding creative ways to connect with him and know him. It's listening to biblical teaching while I'm cleaning up toys, singing praise songs in the car with my children, praying throughout the day, and remembering to talk about him in the everyday moments.

If you are sometimes stressed and tired, waiting for the perfect time to meet with God, remember that there is no requirement for you to only meet with God in the quiet. He knows your season, Mom; he'll meet you where you're at.

BECAUSE YOUR THEOLOGY MATTERS

EMILY

Mama, your theology matters.

No, it doesn't feel like it makes any difference when you are sleep deprived, bouncing a fussy infant, sending a disobedient toddler to time-out, picking Cheerio crumbs out of your rug, or wiping up a potty-training accident. But is that really the case?

Have you ever stopped to think about how your theology—the beliefs you hold about God and his ways—is a subconscious guide that directs what you do? What you think about God—who he is, what he's about, and what he's created you to do—touches every facet of your mundane life.

It helps determine whether you roll your eyes at your laundry pile or humbly complete your unseen work as you meditate on restoring order to your little corner of creation.

It helps determine whether you blow up at your naughty preschooler or pause and pray as you remember how often you've disobeyed your own Father in heaven.

It helps determine whether you choose to spend your time on things that you think you deserve or view all your time as the Lord's, knowing that he is the guide that sets your priorities for the day.

Mama, your theology is the funnel through which you siphon truth from your social media news feed, your book club, your friend's advice, your favorite Christian writer, and the world around you.

And if your theology is undeveloped and mostly based on what you approve of and what generally seems right to you, you will miss the goodness and holiness of God.

You will miss the real truth, the real purpose for your life, and the real gospel-power available to you through the Spirit and the Word.

Mama, cultivate good theology. Don't settle for what someone else tells you about who God is—know him yourself, study his Word yourself, and find the best treasure you could ever imagine.

WHEN YOU DON'T THINK YOU
CAN HAVE A QUIET TIME

LAURA

There's a myth about quiet times we need to talk about. A myth that tells us we need coffee in a handmade mug, a pretty candle, a beautiful notebook with an inspiring quote on the front, and—this is the kicker—at least thirty minutes of uninterrupted quiet time before dawn.

Helllllllo, you're a mom. You might be able to get those first few items together, but you live life in five-minute increments before another need arises—why do you expect your quiet time to be any different? Yes, some days, some seasons, with solid planning and cooperative children, you may get that. And I hope that you do.

But for many of you, right now? In the season of little, tiny, immediate needs? The "perfect" quiet-time circumstances probably won't align that often.

And that's okay. The thing is, Jesus meets you where you're at. Even if that's next to sticky toddler hands and tiny baby toes with the TV playing in the background and a dirty diaper that you have to change midway through. The blanket, candle, mug, or silence aren't what make your quiet time effective. They don't make God any more real or powerful or amazing. While at times, getting your hands on a beautiful new journal can be just the ticket for inspiration and motivation, in reality, it doesn't change the impact a quiet time has to transform your life. All you need is a humble heart, ready and willing to engage with the Word. That's it! When you're in Christ, you can know that the Spirit is at work in you as you read.

As a mom, I've come to realize I need Jesus, all the time, as much as possible, every chance I get. Meeting with Jesus isn't confined to a single part of my day. Not being able to burn a candle because my toddler might knock it over and burn the house down isn't a reason to throw in the towel and not spend time intentionally focused on God and his Word that day.

Every day as a mom is different, but Jesus stays the same. He understands the season you're in and doesn't mind the interruptions, chaos, or noise as you strive to learn more about him in the time you have available.

So today, as hard as it may feel, make time to spend with Jesus. We need him, all the time, every day—whether we have a candle burning or not.

BECAUSE "I'LL DO IT TOMORROW" IS A LIE

EMILY

"I'll read God's Word tomorrow."
"I'll have more self-control tomorrow."
"I'll be kinder to my children tomorrow."
"I'll be more consistent with training and discipline tomorrow."
"I'll do" and "tomorrow" are staples in my mental vocabulary, giving me a false sense of power, security, and dominion over my flesh.

The lie of "I'll do..." is that in my own efforts, by my own intelligence and savvy, I can muster up the ability to create lasting change. It's thinking that I'm able to wake up one day and be different, just because I want to be. It's living in the delusion that I can overcome the desires of my flesh without God's help.

The lie of "tomorrow..." is that I'm in control of time and don't live by human limitations. Although the missteps of others need to be stopped immediately, I can do mine for a little longer without really reaping any serious consequences. It's presuming God's grace, making it cheap for my own convenience. It's thinking that I'm in charge of what happens tomorrow and believing it's guaranteed to be there.

Instead of "I'll do it tomorrow," I want to walk in God's ways here and now. To practice immediate repentance when I feel my heart resisting him and longing to live for myself. I want conviction to stop me in my tracks, acknowledge my inability, and cry out for his help. Not "I'll do it tomorrow," but "Help me to follow you, today."

WHEN YOU WANT TO SEE CHANGE

LAURA

There is a real, spiritual, cosmic battle going on, and it's a fight for you to stop looking at Jesus and to look at *anything else*. If you want to go to battle in this—if you want to see a pattern of sin change, your child's soul change, your husband's heart change, or the world change—you need to start going to war through prayer. You need to fight on your knees.

WHEN WE SPOT A WEED

————————

EMILY

The heat of the summer is not just pool season; it's weed season. When the kids tiptoe from the van to the house dripping with water and wrapped in towels, I scowl at the rogue stems growing up between my flowers. I feel sure they weren't there yesterday. The idea of staying on top of pokey, pesky greenery used to keep me from planting anything beautiful.

When I stuck my trowel in the soil to plant flowers this year, I decided to do things differently. I was going to attack the weeds immediately. Bent down with pincher fingers hovering above well-saturated soil, I'd grab them before they went deep. The small piles of weeds fit in my palm. Tiny pulls every day. With small, consistent efforts, good growth takes center stage.

This is also what I'm learning about repentance (even though it's more pesky and painful than pulling a small weed). At times, I've been so busy that I neglect to deal with sin. Instead of "tiny pulls every day," eventually, I need a major reset.

Maybe you're like me—your hands are full of pool toys, library books, dishes, and diapers. You'll deal with the Lord another day. Maybe over the long holiday weekend? Later next week? You spot sin out of the corner of your eye, but…people need you.

Oh, friend. Let's pull sin today. When a sprout of unrighteous anger, bitterness, unforgiveness, gossip, slander, favoritism, or selfishness sprouts above the surface, let's immediately confess it to the Lord and ask him to tear it away. Let's have the tough conversation or steer our mothering in the right direction. Let's pause and pursue the One who saves us from sin.

With a well-saturated heart, soaked with Scripture, we can readily spot weeds and ask him to hold our trembling hands, bringing whatever is below the surface above ground. Our children can also walk beside us as we teach them how to take their own sin to God through Christ.

Weeds take work, but the chief Gardener goes with us.

FOR CREATIVE SPIRITUAL GROWTH

EMILY

For every mom of little ones who is longing to see her relationship with God as bigger than the elusive "quiet time," this list is for you:

Listen

Consume the Word of God throughout your day by utilizing technology to learn and grow. Use a Bible app and listen to large swaths of Scripture, or put a passage you're trying to memorize on repeat. When you are busy playing with children or cleaning up toys, let rich hymns remind you of important truths. Mundane tasks are a wonderful opportunity to let your mind process through challenging sermons, theological podcasts, or even a good audiobook. Regardless of the time or place, turn on your device and learn as your children soak up the good truth alongside you!

Watch

Beyond just listening, there are archives full of conference messages, speaking engagements, and sermons at your fingertips. Fold laundry with your laptop open to an encouraging or challenging message. Go beyond your favorite Netflix show, and catch up on something that will point you to Jesus. Or you can even catch up on live videos on Facebook by following people who inspire you to take up your cross and spread the gospel.

Read

Most of us are guilty of spending a little too much time on social media, scanning through endless updates, when our time and mind could be better utilized. Have some great books loaded on your Kindle, and train yourself to default there in a down moment instead of to mindless entertainment. Be intentional about who you follow on social media as well, so you can skim or read gospel-centered articles instead of just cultural inspiration.

Share

As you learn, turn around and share the truth with others, even your kids if they are around. You might feel like you sound a bit crazy at first, but they will eventually get used to hearing Mom verbally process theological truths. Grow in your comfort level with gospel conversations by engaging a friend who is willing to ping-pong doctrinal ideas back and forth. Share with anyone you can reach or who will listen, through social media, in conversations over coffee, or even with your husband as you clean up the house at bedtime. When you can share what you're learning in an understandable way, you can be confident the truths are being etched deeply on your heart.

Pray

Finally (and this one is hard for many of us), give yourself lots of opportunities to pray throughout the day. They don't have to be long, quiet, complex prayers but moments to acknowledge your need for God and your gratitude for his grace. I find these to be natural occurrences at mealtimes, rest times, and times of correction for young children. As you pray the truths you're learning from your listening, watching, reading, and sharing—alone and with your children—you'll see opportunities and praise God more readily for them.

WHEN IT FEELS IMPOSSIBLE TO MEET WITH JESUS

LAURA

If you're like me, you've looked at moms that have written about how they made daily time for meeting with God and wondered how they can possibly find time to be in the Word. As moms, our lives change quickly. Rarely does one day look like the next. And even when we set aside time in the early morning hours before our children typically wake up, things happen. Kids get sick, they wake up early, we go on trips. Moms have a lot of "seasons within a season" of life, so consistency is genuinely hard.

But being in the Word is how we connect with God. It's one of the main ways for us to discover what he loves and cares about and learn about his plan for our lives, and it's a tool he uses to transform us more into the image of Christ. All this to say, it's worth it to prioritize reading the Word, Mom.

Here are a few things I've learned about having a regular quiet time, no matter the season you're in.

Find a Consistent Time

Finding a reliable time truly does help make quiet time a habit. Many people find waking up earlier than their kids is best. But if your kids are up all night or routinely wake at 5 a.m., try to find another part of the day that typically works—nap time, before bed, on the train to work. Don't feel like you have to structure your day like anyone else's. Do what works for your schedule. You can even consider having two or three "spots" in your mind where you can squeeze it in, moving it around depending on your day.

Prepare for Distractions

Step back and think through anything that might pull your attention away from the Lord. Things like your phone, the TV, or music. Within the first couple of days of doing an intentional quiet time, you'll figure out your distractions. Don't let them set you off track. Of course, as a mom, there may be distractions that you can't avoid. You may have children around, dinner cooking, a neighbor coming to the door. That's okay. Remember, the Lord knows your season; he's not annoyed by it.

Put Things Close at Hand

It's an old trick, but it works. Keeping everything together in a central spot both gives you a visual cue about the habit you're trying to build and takes away the barrier of having to hunt everything down. Put all the things you like to use—like your Bible, a Bible study book, a journal for quiet-time notes, a prayer journal, pens and highlighters, and so on—all together in a basket in a place you know you'll see.

Have a Plan

Know what you'd like to study before you start. Some people prefer a formal Bible study with accountability, others like reading through the Bible in a year, and still others like journaling through a passage of Scripture. You can do one of those things, or all three! Just know in advance what your plan is so you're not scrambling when you finally sit down.

Get Accountability

Swap emails or audio messages about what you've read, send each other texts to let each other know you've done it, or even have a weekly playdate to discuss what you're learning. Accountability is a great way to grow with others and to motivate you on those days it's hard to find the desire for it.

Ask God to Help You

Pray and ask God to make the desire to have a quiet time with him burn brightly in your heart. God longs to spend time with you, and anytime you ask for more of him, he honors that request. Just ask!

Remember: There Are No True Rules!

At the end of the day, there are no rules for quiet times. It's between you and the Lord. Don't compare what you're doing to anyone else. Allow the Lord to direct your thoughts and your time. Some days, you really will just have ten minutes. Other days, you'll have an hour. You can trust that God will guide you in the right things to study, bring the right things to mind, and allow the truth you need to hear to stand out with the time and energy you have.

WHEN YOU DON'T THINK IT'S POSSIBLE TO SABBATH

LAURA

"What are you doing for Sabbath rest?" my sister-in-law asked me. After sharing how overwhelmed I felt in this season of raising young children, I laughed. "Sabbath? I don't have time for a Sabbath!" I replied.

A few minutes later, she told me to open my phone to a Venn diagram. With a few strokes of a pen, she had mapped out all my major commitments, how they overlapped, and the deeper heart issues they revealed. Although I didn't ask her to, she took the liberty to itemize my life and point out, in love, that I was overcommitted, striving, and needed rest.

Over the course of several days, conversations, and prayer, I realized I didn't just need the kind of rest where I kick my feet up; I needed the deep soul rest that comes from dependence on Christ and is commanded by God: Sabbath rest. Out of his goodness and mercy, God rested from his work on the seventh day of creation (Genesis 2:15), setting a pattern for his creatures to follow.

I realized I needed a new definition of rest.

The Sabbath is an essential break from our normal work. More importantly, though, it's a spiritual rest; we remember that as God's people, we are to be like him, set apart and made holy in Christ. When we rest, we imitate

God. We remember the Lord of our salvation and focus our delight and joy in him and his accomplished work, not our own.

Discipline in Gospel Trust

I'll rest after I get a little more done, I say to myself while washing dishes, doing laundry, and paying bills. We often feel better resting when we know dinner is in the crockpot and the toys are picked up. Sabbath may be a day of rest, we think, but I'll rest when I'm done with all this.

This faulty line of thinking is rooted in a deeper belief that the success of life and motherhood depends on ourselves. We're not just working on a completed to-do list; we're working on achieving "good mom status." We're afraid to rest because we don't trust God to rule over our world—or at least, do it the way we would.

Yet in Christ, our striving for "good-mom status" was nailed to the cross. When Jesus defeated death, he deemed us righteous, loved, and accepted. It's because of Christ's actions—not ours—that we find our rest in the Lord rather than in a completed to-do list.

There will always be unfinished tasks in the home, but taking time for Sabbath is a necessary discipline in gospel trust as we outwardly embody our inward reliance on Christ. It's not something we'll get to "later"—that day, or in a few years when the kids are older. The Sabbath is a weekly reminder that only God holds the world together, even when we stop.

Working Hands, Resting Heart

For many of us, once we choose to prioritize a Sabbath, our natural tendency is to define it by our rules: no computer, no paying bills, no errands. Go on a walk, take a nap, read a book. But what happens when the baby gets sick, or the nap-time revolt begins, or we hear about a neighbor who needs help? What happens to Sabbath rest when the work of life gets in the way?

When it comes to the Sabbath, there's a Pharisee lurking in us all. Just like the self-righteous people of Jesus's day, we want to focus on legislation. But Christ shows us a better way. In the Gospels, Jesus makes clear our highest priority should be to love God and our neighbor, even on the Jewish Sabbath. When the Pharisees called Jesus out on the Sabbath for plucking grain from the field and for healing a withered man's hand, he responded, "I desire mercy, and not sacrifice" (Matthew 12:7), and just a few verses later, "Do good on the Sabbath" (Matthew 12:12).

The essence of Sabbath rest isn't found in the terms of our do-and-don't lists. Instead, we remember weekly that our God is holy, and as his people, we are to be the same. When we Sabbath with this in mind, our hands may "do good" while our hearts continue to rest in the good news of the gospel.

That means sometimes the Sabbath looks like momma getting a nap, and sometimes it looks like washing soiled sheets. Sometimes it looks like reading a book, and sometimes it looks like bringing a meal to someone at church. When Jesus is our rest, it can be a day of showing mercy and love, being in the mess, making sacrifices, and being content with the inefficiencies of young children. It can be a day of high cost to ourselves, in order to show Jesus to others.

That's because our weekly rest isn't about tightly kept boundaries; it's about delighting and finding our joy in the Lord. As we spend our Sabbath going to church with our fellow saints, taking time for personal Bible reading and study, or heading outdoors for a prayer walk, we deepen our dependence on Christ. As mothers, we can bring our children alongside us—telling them Bible stories, practicing Scripture memory, or bringing them with us as we visit the sick and needy—to teach them the regular rhythms of a believer and reveal a mother wholly reliant on God, not her own efforts.

Live like His Word Is True

I often think back to that Venn diagram of my life. Since then, some circles have shifted, new ones have been added, and others have disappeared entirely. It's a reminder that life is always changing, but our God is not. Christ came and completed all the necessary work for us. It is finished.

It's possible to make the Sabbath a day of rest, even in the season of young children. If you're working with no rest, stop and repent. Believe God is who he says he is. Live like Jesus's words are really true: "Come to me, all who labor and are heavy laden, and I will give you rest" (Matthew 11:28).

WHEN WE NEED AFFIRMATION

LAURA

The question we need to ask is, Are we doing this for God's glory or ours? Do we trust God to reward us even in secret? Do we think that we need others' affirmation to keep going? For people to say, "Wow, look at her, look at how amazing she is!" Or do you have a genuine heart to steward well what you've been given, even if only the Lord sees?

BECAUSE GOSPEL GROWTH
CAN HAPPEN ANYWHERE

EMILY

With four young children, a moment of quiet or predictable consistency is hard to come by. Even with my best efforts to be organized and intentional, it's still difficult to stay engaged in regular Bible study, to disciple women, to fellowship regularly with other believers, or to serve in ways that pull me out of my home. The desire is there, but so are the dirty diapers, the nap-time routines, the laundry piles, and the mundane things that keep our family going.

All the distractions, setbacks, and challenges occasionally leave me wondering if theological growth just isn't possible in the season of young children. I've wondered if I should just shrug at my inconsistent quiet times and parched prayer life.

But by God's mercy, I've also seen that a life apart from frequent fellowship with Jesus is bleak at best. The Lord has broadened my view to see creative ways to grow in my knowledge of sound doctrine, rich theology, and gospel truth (even when laundry mountains and full crockpots abound). I've learned to use the gift of technology to learn and grow—listening to the audio Bible, theologically rich podcasts, and solid sermons. I've learned to stop the scroll, set down social media, and pick up my Bible (even in the middle of the afternoon). I've learned to "sneak prayer in" by pairing it with regular daily activities like going on a walk with the kids or washing the dishes. And when I stay connected to the vine in this way, I've also noticed that it's easier to see God's hand and work and respond to his leading each day.

Regardless of how you consume and pour out gospel truth, the key is to immerse yourself. Be obsessed with learning about and loving Jesus. Stop viewing time with the Lord as limited to a moment in your favorite chair with your favorite coffee mug when all is quiet before the kids wake. While that is wonderful—and moms often need more moments to be alone with God—that doesn't invalidate the thousands of other opportunities to love the Lord with all your heart, soul, mind, and strength throughout the day.

Mom, catch a bigger vision of gospel growth that includes your children, mundane chores, workday commutes, meals, and times of fellowship. Theology is for you, too, even if you have a baby on your hip and a toddler at your knees.

FOR WHEN YOU NEED PRACTICAL HELP WITH KIDS

Whatever you are speaking over your children—
no matter their abilities, no matter how God
made them physically, no matter what they can
do—speak this: God loves his children, God made
his children, and God is kind to his children.

LAURA

WHEN YOU DON'T
KNOW WHAT TO DO

_____

EMILY

I'd pretty much exhausted all my usual strategies when I came to my husband and said, "I'm just out of ideas for how to handle this behavior. What should I do?"

(I was listening intently for a magic bullet that I hadn't thought of yet. I really wanted a three-step solution to correct the heart attitude of our preschooler.)

"Well, have you tried praying with him? Let him see that you are both dependent on the Lord for a change."

All at once, relief and frustration flooded over me. One part of my mind scolded the suggestion, "_Prayer_?! How is that going to help when I'm at the end of my rope? I need something practical I can implement!"

But the deepest part of my heart relented, "Yes. _Prayer_. Because I don't have the answers, I can't change my son's heart, and I want to model deep dependence on God for help and solutions. God will give wisdom. He will meet me there."

How often do we feel this way? We parent our little ones, day in and day out, growing disillusioned with all the foolproof discipline strategies promised to us on the internet and in books. We put our hope in the methods alone, thinking that if we just do enough research or execute it more perfectly, then maybe we can finally have control over our children. While God works in and through a myriad of parenting strategies, and they are good to research and implement, we mustn't forget the cross.

If our children came with a handbook, a set of easy-to-do strategies, we wouldn't need God. We would quickly depend on our own efforts and tell our children to do the same.

We—mothers and children—are both leveled at the cross.

Both dependent.

Both needy.

Both desperate to be rescued, guided, and loved.

And in the absence of a perfect "this is how we are going to move forward" plan, we can at least show our children whom we look to and depend on for help. We can pray.

FOR TALKING TO YOUR KIDS ABOUT GOD IN EVERYDAY LIFE

EMILY

Even if we're not used to talking about God with other people, talking to our children about God can become one of the most natural, low-stakes ways to enter in. Conversations about God don't have to be scheduled or awkward—there are numerous ways we can naturally weave thoughts about the Lord into our everyday lives. Here are ten opportunities to strike up a conversation about God with your kids (along with related Scriptures for each one). Depending on the ages and stages of your kids, these verses might be appropriate to share with them if the conversation allows, and they'll definitely help prepare your own heart and mind!

1. When they see something they love in nature, remind them that God created everything.

   Genesis 1:1: "In the beginning, God created the heavens and the earth."

   Nehemiah 9:6: "You are the LORD, you alone. You have made heaven, the heaven of heavens, with all their host, the earth and all that is on it, the seas and all that is in them; and you preserve all of them; and the host of heaven worships you."

John 1:1-3: "In the beginning was the Word, and the Word was with God, and the Word was God. He was in the beginning with God. All things were made through him, and without him was not any thing made that was made."

2. When they get ready to eat a meal, encourage them to give thanks to God for all he provides.

   Psalm 136:25: "He who gives food to all flesh, for his steadfast love endures forever."

   Matthew 6:11-12: "Give us this day our daily bread, and forgive us our debts, as we also have forgiven our debtors."

3. When they show off a skill, gift, or ability, tell them that God gives us abilities to glorify and worship him.

   Exodus 31:1-6: "The LORD said to Moses, 'See, I have called by name Bezalel the son of Uri, son of Hur, of the tribe of Judah, and I have filled him with the Spirit of God, with ability and intelligence, with knowledge and all craftsmanship, to devise artistic designs, to work in gold, silver, and bronze, in cutting stones for setting, and in carving wood, to work in every craft. And behold, I have appointed with him Oholiab, the son of Ahisamach, of the tribe of Dan. And I have given to all able men ability, that they may make all that I have commanded you."

Ecclesiastes 9:10: "Whatever your hand finds to do, do it with your might, for there is no work or thought or knowledge or wisdom in Sheol, to which you are going."

Colossians 3:23-24: "Whatever you do, work heartily, as for the Lord and not for men, knowing that from the Lord you will receive the inheritance as your reward. You are serving the Lord Christ."

4. **When they get hurt or feel afraid, remind them that God is always with us; he is our refuge and strength.**

Psalm 34:4-7: "I sought the LORD, and he answered me and delivered me from all my fears. Those who look to him are radiant, and their faces shall never be ashamed. This poor man cried, and the LORD heard him and saved him out of all his troubles. The angel of the LORD encamps around those who fear him, and delivers them."

Psalm 56:3-4: "When I am afraid, I put my trust in you. In God, whose word I praise, in God I trust; I shall not be afraid. What can flesh do to me?"

Philippians 4:6-7: "Do not be anxious about anything, but in everything by prayer and supplication with thanksgiving let your requests be made known to God. And the peace of God, which surpasses all understanding, will guard your hearts and your minds in Christ Jesus."

5. **When they disobey, share that sin has broken our relationship with God, but he offers forgiveness in his Son, Jesus.**

   Psalm 130:3-4: "If you, O LORD, should mark iniquities, O Lord, who could stand? But with you there is forgiveness, that you may be feared."

   Ephesians 2:8-9: "For by grace you have been saved through faith. And this is not your own doing; it is the gift of God, not a result of works, so that no one may boast."

   1 John 1:9: "If we confess our sins, he is faithful and just to forgive us our sins and to cleanse us from all unrighteousness."

6. **When they see you reading the Bible or praying, let them know that God wants us to spend time getting to know him.**

   Psalm 1:2: "But his delight is in the law of the LORD, and on his law he meditates day and night."

   Psalm 119:15-17: "I will meditate on your precepts and fix my eyes on your ways. I will delight in your statutes; I will not forget your word. Deal bountifully with your servant, that I may live and keep your word."

   1 Thessalonians 5:16-18: "Rejoice always, pray without ceasing, give thanks in all circumstances; for this is the will of God in Christ Jesus for you."

7. **When they hurt others, remind them that God created everyone in his image and he wants us to be kind to others.**

   Genesis 1:26-27: "Then God said, 'Let us make man in our image, after our likeness. And let them have dominion over the fish of the sea and over the birds of the heavens and over the livestock and over all the earth and over every creeping thing that creeps on the earth.' So God created man in his own image, in the image of God he created him; male and female he created them."

   Ephesians 4:32: "Be kind to one another, tenderhearted, forgiving one another, as God in Christ forgave you."

   1 Thessalonians 5:11: "Therefore encourage one another and build one another up, just as you are doing."

8. **When they share or show generosity, point out how much God loves a cheerful giver.**

   2 Corinthians 9:6-7: "The point is this: whoever sows sparingly will also reap sparingly, and whoever sows bountifully will also reap bountifully. Each one must give as he has decided in his heart, not reluctantly or under compulsion, for God loves a cheerful giver."

   Hebrews 10:34: "For you had compassion on those in prison, and you joyfully accepted the plundering of your property, since you knew that you yourselves had a better possession and an abiding one."

9. When they show self-control instead of selfishness, rejoice in how God helped them do what is right and show love to others.

1 Corinthians 13:4-5: "Love is patient and kind; love does not envy or boast; it is not arrogant or rude. It does not insist on its own way; it is not irritable or resentful."

Galatians 5:22-23: "But the fruit of the Spirit is love, joy, peace, patience, kindness, goodness, faithfulness, gentleness, self-control; against such things there is no law."

10. When they are ready for bed, tell them that God loves them, is with them, and hears their prayers.

Psalm 4:8: "In peace I will both lie down and sleep; for you alone, O LORD, make me dwell in safety."

James 5:13: "Is anyone among you suffering? Let him pray. Is anyone cheerful? Let him sing praise."

1 John 5:14-15: "And this is the confidence that we have toward him, that if we ask anything according to his will he hears us. And if we know that he hears us in whatever we ask, we know that we have the requests that we have asked of him."

WHEN YOU DON'T KNOW WHAT TO TEACH YOUR CHILDREN ABOUT GOD

EMILY

When my son was just about a year old, I heard a mom friend say that she was doing Scripture memory with her three-year-old because he was "such a sponge." I remember feeling intimidated and wondered if I was behind. *Should I be doing more Scripture memory with my baby?* (I literally thought that, even though he couldn't talk yet!) It would have been great for me to start reading the Scriptures over him, knowing that those words can root themselves early. But instead of focusing on the little things and the long road, making it a goal to consistently expose him to the Word of God, I started to make teaching my child about God scary and complicated. I felt apprehensive about methods and strategies. I was anxious about what would happen if I "failed" to dive into all the habits of grace with him as quickly as possible.

The question about what to teach our children—Scripture memory? catechisms? missionary biographies? vocabulary words?—can feel complex and intimidating, but it's also simple.

Teach them to do what you do and know what you know. And then, push all your boundaries even further. Consistently expose them to God's Word and prayer. Let it seep into every corner of family life until it's the very thing that upholds your life. Learn to use enriching tools and engage in helpful spiritual disciplines as a family as you grow together.

Let them see you authentically loving God, repenting when you fail, turning to God in prayer, and studying sound doctrine along with the local church. Involve them when you host neighbors for dinner, encourage them to work hard when no one is looking, and love them as image-bearers of God. No doubt, it's hard to be faithful in this work, but *what* to teach them is actually fairly simple. Teach them to be a follower of Christ.

Years have passed. Five kids later, I'm still getting my sea legs under me in terms of Bible teaching and children, but I've realized that it's a long road of discipleship that will involve different tools and strategies at different times. But at all times, when I keep the love of God, his people, and his Word at the center, it's not so complicated after all.

FOR SPEAKING LIFE-GIVING WORDS TO YOUR CHILDREN

EMILY

Children chant, "Sticks and stones may break my bones, but words will never hurt me." But as moms, we know better. Words are powerful. Words can build up, and words can tear down. Day by day and moment by moment, we have opportunities to speak life-giving words to our children, to encourage and equip, to impart wisdom and hope. But it can feel awkward getting started and knowing what to say. So here are a few natural times that you can practice today.

When they are imaging Jesus: *"You are helping and serving. Thank you!"*

Because we long to raise our children to follow God's ways, our tendency can sometimes be to emphasize where our children are out of alignment with his Word, while their childlike joy, or efforts to help and serve may go unacknowledged. Making an intentional effort to point out the positives can be a tremendous encouragement for both kids and moms.

When they make the choice to obey: *"God helped you keep your hands in the cart at the store like Mommy asked!"*

We all have to struggle against our sinful nature to make choices that honor the Lord. When our children obey, we have an opportunity to help them understand that God helps us in our struggle against sin and his Spirit bears fruit in our lives. Be specific about how you see the Lord helping them grow in obedience.

When they need biblical wisdom: *"Remember, whoever loves God must also love his brother. This is hard, but God can help you be kind!"*

Begin building a foundation of biblical wisdom in your children by regularly speaking and applying basic truths from Scripture in everyday life. Start with foundational truths about loving God and loving others that will apply to many situations.

When they are afraid or unsure: *"I know you feel scared. Remember, God is always with you."*

Some of our children's fears can be easily explained away, but they also deal with real fears, and we can't guarantee that everything will be fine. However, we can encourage them with the promises of Scripture. Over and over, God tells his people not to fear because he will always be with us and he's working for our ultimate good.

When they are headed to nap or bedtime: *"Mommy loves you so much. I'm so glad God put you in our family."*

We can never tell our children too many times that we love them and are thankful for them! And even in subtle ways, we can begin to teach them that God is sovereign over all things and doesn't make mistakes. We can affirm his good design and purposes in putting our family together as we convey that they are a good gift from the Lord.

When you notice a gift or special ability: *"God created you with such a wonderful imagination. I can't wait to see how you use that to help others someday!"*

When we see our children succeed, it can be easy to feel pride in ourselves and encourage it in our children. But when their strengths and talents are on display, we have an opportunity to point them to the One who gave them those abilities and begin to teach them to look for ways to use their gifts to serve God and others.

When you notice an area of weakness: *"It's hard to use nice words, but God can help change your heart and your words."*

Just as God has compassion on us in our sin, we can show compassion to our children. When they struggle, we can affirm that fighting against sin is hard. And we can point them to the hope of the gospel—that the power to overcome sin doesn't come from ourselves but from Christ's work on the cross.

Of course, your words don't have to sound exactly like these, and the opportunities for speaking life are much wider. But hopefully these ideas can get you started!

FOR TEACHING YOUR KIDS TO PRAY

LAURA

One day, while I was teaching Sunday school to a room full of first-graders, a tiny hand shot into the air. Without pausing for me to call on her, she asked, "If God hears me pray, why doesn't he talk back to me?" Her big round eyes stared at me earnestly, and I instantly felt out of my depth. How was I going to explain this to a room of six- and seven-year-olds who were—for the first time all morning—quiet and attentive as they waited for my answer?

As a mom to three children, I'm struck by how many questions my kids have about prayer. As my husband and I have tried to develop a culture of prayer in our home, it's also provided a springboard for conversations about what it means to talk with God. Which, in turn, has created space for us to lay a solid theological foundation for many related topics. Here are four foundational truths about prayer (and therefore God) we consistently come back to.

God Can Always Hear Us

"Can God hear me in my mind?" My six-year-old randomly asked me this while we were baking cookies recently. It's a good question, so I took her to Scripture: Psalm 6:9, "The LORD has heard my plea for help; the LORD accepts my prayer," and Psalm 139:4, "Before a word is on my tongue, you know all about it, LORD" (CSB).

When talking to our kids about prayer, we can show them how Scripture tells us God hears us no matter where we are or what we're doing. Whether whispered at the store, yelled in a gym, or thought silently in their mind at school, God always hears the prayers of his people because of Jesus. Christ lived a perfect life on earth and made a way for us to talk with God by paying for our sins on the cross. In fact, today Jesus is in heaven, praying for us (Romans 8:34)! It's because of Christ that no matter where his people are or what they're doing, God is always delighted to hear from them.

God Always Answers Our Prayers

Just like the little girl in my Sunday school class, a typical follow-up question to understanding if God hears our prayers is, "Then why can't I hear him?" One of the things I'm still learning as an adult is that God is not "like me." He doesn't do things the same way humans do, and it's an important concept to talk to our children about as well.

Teach your children that God does talk to us, but it's different from how they hear from their friends or parents. Generally, God speaks to us through his Word and by the Holy Spirit. The old adage "God always answers with either a yes, no, or not now" is helpful here. Prayer isn't like rubbing Aladdin's lamp and having the genie grant every request we want. It's primarily meant to change our own hearts to align with God's and to teach us to depend on him (2 Corinthians 9:8). As they grow older, you can help your child understand that God can see things they can't, and if they understood everything, they'd answer the same way he does (Proverbs 3:5). We pray not to get what we want but to get more of him. And that request is always answered with a "yes."

There Is Nothing Too Big or Small for God

When our children pray for "the dog to have a good day" over and over, we as parents can start to wonder, "Is it okay if my kids pray to a holy God like this? Is this somehow sacrilegious?" Take heart that prayers like this are completely normal for young children. It's a wonderful thing for them to know that they really can bring any request to the God who cares for the sparrows and numbers the hairs on their head (Luke 12:6-7).

Over time, lift your child's eyes to see all the different things they can pray about. Show them prayers from Scripture that help them see the ways God's people have prayed throughout history. Talk with them about real people in your family's life and things they can pray for, or ask your child about their hopes and dreams and encourage them to pray about those. Help your child see that prayer is so much more than simply saying generalities or repeating something they heard you say but that they can pray in particulars, both big and small (Philippians 4:6).

God Wants Us to Come as We Are

As children grow older, they typically become more aware and self-conscious of how they pray. Help them see that prayer isn't something they need to clean up for, have warm and fuzzy feelings about, or get perfectly right. Prayer isn't an otherworldly activity where they need a special incantation or a poetic display like the Pharisee in Luke 10. It's about authentically talking with God, truthfully pouring out cares, desires, needs, and dreams like the tax collector. If they don't know what to say, teach them how the Spirit intercedes for them, even when they don't know what to pray for (Romans 8:26). Because of Christ, they can come just as they are (Romans 15:7). It's okay if it's been a long time since they've remembered to pray, and it's definitely okay if they seem to pray without ceasing! Of course, over time we all can learn and grow in our understanding and methods for prayer, but it's most important for our prayers to be true, honest, and humble, focused on God's glory and our love of him.

Above all, remember that "more is caught than taught." As you make prayer a regular rhythm in your family's daily life, your children will naturally see how these foundations are true. So more than talking to our children about prayer, may we be moms who pray in front of and for our children, asking God to grow in them a love and joy for talking with him.

WHEN YOU WANT TO EXPLAIN DISABILITIES TO YOUR CHILDREN

_____

LAURA

Our home is at the end of a cul-de-sac, and because our neighborhood was built on an old Iowa cornfield, it backs up to the only thin band of woods that runs along one side of the development. The neighboring children are naturally drawn to the trees, which means there might be anywhere from five to twenty kids playing in our yard at any given time. Racing around on scooters or roller blades, stomping up from the creek with muddy boots, or walking back from our tree fort shouting about the bugs they caught in a jar—it's everything I've ever wanted in a neighborhood.

But sometimes, the sight of all the happy kids running around pricks my heart in pain. Because of disabilities, my daughter can't visit the woods without my help. She can't keep pace with the scooters in the driveway, and she can't easily communicate about the treasures she's found.

Sometimes my kids ask why their sister seems different from the other children in our life. I'll never forget the time my oldest asked pointedly, "Why did God make her like that?" It struck me like a gust of wind on a cold Iowa day, knowing this was the question I was looking to answer as well.

Thankfully, the Bible isn't silent on this topic. Here are four theological truths I've shared with my children to help them understand God's design in allowing one of their siblings to have disabilities.

1. God made all of us in his image. Genesis 1:26 tells us that when God created people, he said, "Let us make man in our image, after our likeness." The words "image" and "likeness" speak of every person's resemblance to God, giving all of us equal dignity and value. This means, no matter our abilities, we all carry the stamp of God on us. We're not duplicates of one another, but because we're a family, there is a sameness (Galatians 3:28-29). Help your children see that just as every person in the family has different abilities and gifts, each is equally valuable and loved.

2. The Fall affects everyone. At the same time, the world is broken. The Fall affects everyone and everything. It's not hard to help your child see that the world is broken. A toy breaks when it drops to the floor, a sibling shoves to get a better view, the baby birds fall from the nest. Adam's sin has affected everything—nothing is untouched.

Help your children see that when it comes to disabilities, more often than not, it's simply a result of living in a fallen world (John 9:1-3). Even in cases when disability or delays may be the result of abuse or neglect, we can teach our children to focus on having compassion for others rather than diagnosing who was at fault. Whether we know the reason or not, these things are a part of life east of Eden, and they will be with us until we go home to glory.

3. God is sovereign over how each of us was formed. When we explain that having disabilities is a part of a fallen world, it may feel like disabilities were passed out at random. But we know from Psalm 139 that God made every human intentionally and by his design ("For it was you who created my inward parts; you knit me together in my mother's womb").

Help your children see that just as God intentionally chose their hair color, the size of their feet, and what activities they would excel at, he also formed every limp, every irregular organ, every stutter, and every eye that only sees darkness. "The LORD said to [Moses], 'Who has made man's mouth? Who makes him mute, or deaf, or seeing, or blind? Is it not I, the LORD?'" (Exodus 4:11).

Every chromosome, every gene, every atom—God commands at his will. He makes no mistakes. God is still good and uses disabilities for his purposes.

4. God is still good. Disability is costly—emotionally, physically, and spiritually. Young children in particular don't always have the maturity to filter their experiences. As parents, we can help our children see that God has a perfect purpose in creating their family as he did.

When the disciples had questions about a man born blind, Jesus told them, "This came about so that God's works might be displayed in him" (John 9:3 CSB). Or in Lazarus's sickness, Jesus told his disciples, "It is for the glory of God, so that the Son of God may be glorified through it" (John 11:4). In both cases, Jesus points out that God is glorified through the disability.

Sometimes, particularly for children, this can be hard to see. In our family, we talk about both the joys and difficulties of having a sibling with disabilities. There are times when they'll need to slow down to care for their sister, interpret her vocalizations for friends, or go home early from a fun event so she can rest. As they lay down their lives for their sibling, God uses their sacrifice to sanctify and teach them about his love and their obedience.

We also talk about all the wonderful ways their sister has blessed our family. We talk about how inspiring it is to watch her accomplish new things, her care for them when they're hurt, and—perhaps my favorite—how joyfully she sings worship songs no matter where we are. She gives us a front-row seat to aspects of God we wouldn't have without her. Help your children see God's goodness to them and their sibling with disabilities.

Living with Tension

For siblings and parents, having disabilities is both joy and sorrow, sadness and celebration. As William Cowper wrote, "The bud may have a bitter taste, but sweet will be the flower." It's a tension we must learn to live with. We don't always know God's exact purposes for his ways, but we can trust that our families can "count it all joy" and will "lack nothing" as we walk this journey (James 1:2-4).

As parents, we can emphasize the kindness of God, knowing that "for those who love God all things work together for good" (Romans 8:28). This is God's promise that gives hope to every member in the family who follows Christ.

So the next time our children ask, "Why is she like that?" we can answer genuinely, "I don't know why God chose this, but I trust God with it. God is good to us, and it's part of his purpose for our family."

TO SEE NEEDS AND MEET THEM

LAURA

"See needs and meet them." My mom was known for this phrase as I was growing up. All she had to do was say, "See needs..." and I knew what she was going to say and (more importantly) what she meant. Today, I find myself repeating that phrase to my children. Whether it's someone needing a tissue because they're crying, a cabinet door that needs to be shut, or toys spread across the floor that need to be cleaned up, my prayer for my children is they will grow to be people who see needs, and—instead of waiting for someone to ask them—they are the first to stand up and help without ever being asked.

This simple phrase carries so much weight and meaning for me, and hopefully someday it will for my kids as well, teaching them to be observant of their surroundings, to take initiative, to have empathy for others, to be industrious and hardworking, discerning and attentive. Most importantly, it reminds them to live a life like Jesus's example. To have a servant's heart that loves others more than itself. To see the true needs below the surface—the needs of the heart—and to humbly serve in a way that draws the glory and fame to God and his great works rather than to the work of their own hands.

His fame, not ours.

For a heart that is saved is a heart that serves. And a heart that serves is a heart that acts as the hands and feet of Jesus.

Let us be mothers who teach our children to "see needs and meet them." And not only teach it but live it.

WHEN YOU NEED A MENTOR

EMILY

So many of us entered motherhood feeling totally unequipped for the task, both emotionally and practically. Whether it was questions about how to soothe a gassy infant or questions about how to keep going on days with three hours of sleep, the need for helpers arrives swiftly at the doorstep. With all these insecurities and a real need for guidance, we quickly can find ourselves needing a mentor.

While that sounds good in theory, is it realistic to find a mentor in motherhood? And even if you find someone, how do you approach them, and what should your expectations be?

Although we would love for the woman we admire to "notice" us, the reality is that most women feel busy and inadequate for the task of mentorship. If you see a mom who might make a good mentor for you, consider approaching her and sharing your desire for more wisdom in motherhood. This can take courage, and it might not work out, but it's still worth trying.

When you find a mentor, consider agreeing to meet for a set amount of time, and then have a clear date to reevaluate. It's also helpful to communicate what you want to talk about and determine if there is a resource that would be good to go through together. ("I'd love it if you would read this parenting article with me and give me your thoughts on it.")

Not every mom (or mentor) has time for an intense, drawn-out relationship. But that doesn't mean you can't still seek input from an older, wiser woman. Write down your specific questions, and consider inviting someone over during nap time or out for early morning coffee for a one-time meeting. Give them your questions in advance, and make the most of your short time together. Even this type of interaction can have huge benefits.

God designed us to live in community with other moms and learn wisdom from one another—so seek out those relationships. There isn't one mom who has to fill the whole "mentor" role in your life herself either. Pray for God to provide a variety of moms in different ages and stages of life whom you can go to for support.

WHEN YOU HAVE INCOME-PRODUCING WORK

LAURA

It was on an old notepad that I first wrote "be available" on my to-do list. Slotted between "write the article" and "edit the proposal," "be available" was meant to signal what I valued and hoped to be in my very best moments of motherhood. Work was busier than ever, and because I worked from home, my job consistently bled out of its boundaries. It didn't help that I loved my work: the measurable productivity, the opportunities, the obvious and quick results—whether by nature, by nurture, by grace, or by sin, these were my natural bent and my work was their playground.

But I also had three small humans who depended on me. That dependence required slowing down, feeling unproductive, saying no to opportunities, and waiting years for results. It required everything I felt I was not. So "be available" went on the to-do list. (Since God had made me task oriented, I would find a way to redeem it.) Each day, when my nanny left and I picked up my son from school, I decided to shut my laptop until bedtime. I wouldn't do housework (except for making supper—which included both destroying and cleaning up the kitchen). I wouldn't do paperwork, run errands, or take a personal call unless absolutely required. My job, at 3:15 p.m. each day, was to be available for my children.

I built Legos, colored pictures, and made bracelets. I played Sleeping Queens, War, and Pretty Princess. I was bored sometimes. I laughed harder than I ever thought was possible with children that young. I was doing it. I was being a good mom! I was accomplishing things at work! I was balancing it all!

Then I hit some pressing deadlines for work. I pushed off the request to make cookies with my daughter, flipped on a TV show for all three, and sat down in the other room with my laptop. As I sent out emails as fast as I could, I berated my inability to "be available" for even a few weeks. The high crashed, and I felt guilty for not being fully present with my children. For not doing what I thought a good mom would. For being inadequate and insufficient—unable.

Truth: You will never find the perfect balance. At a women's event I attended, someone asked the panel how to find balance as a working mom. One of the panelists got out of her chair and stood on one foot. She bent and rocked, her arms splayed out as she sought to keep one foot in the air. One moment she'd have it, then the next her body swayed like wheat on a windy day. "You see this?" she said. "I'm trying to find balance, but I'm always looking for it. I'm always readjusting." It's a vivid picture I've never forgotten.

I believe there are a handful of golden questions in motherhood, and "How do I find balance?" is one of them. Yet it's as elusive as predicting what your toddler will want to eat for dinner. The reality of life east of Eden means that no matter how we order our days—what we put on our to-do list, what systems we set in place, what things we add or let go of—we won't perfectly meet our self-imposed mark. Scripture tells us all "creation was subjected to futility" (Romans 8:20). This life is a briar patch, tugging and pulling on our best-laid plans. Our inability to strike the balance as mothers is not always a mark of our failure—it's a mark of our humanity on a broken earth. While we need to be good stewards of our time, God isn't asking us to cobble together the perfect formula for a perfectly balanced life; he's asking us to be humble enough to regroup when things aren't working, to walk in the grace purchased for us in Christ, and to remember that "the steps of a [mother] are established by the LORD, when [she] delights in his way" (Psalm 37:23). He knows homes and workplaces are not robotic machines—they are living, breathing spaces that require adjustment, judgment, involvement. Seeking balance isn't the goal—God is.

Truth: Being away from your kids will be hard. My youngest daughter has global developmental delays, which means she's been in physical therapy since she was two months old. We waited three and a half years for her first steps, and I missed them because I was working. Try as I might, I couldn't assuage the pain of wondering if I should have been there. Would it have been okay had I been at the store? At my other child's T-ball game? In the bathroom?

As mothers, we know our children, particularly in the young years, need safety and security in the home. Yet no matter if we work or not, we'll spend time away from them. It's not only necessary (see bathroom) but also healthy. We are people too, and we're creating a foundation from which to launch the little people we're entrusted to raise. Depending on whether work is a necessity or a choice, we may be able to turn the knob up or down on our hours away as we are sensitive to the needs of our children. As we do, we should listen to Scripture, the Spirit working through our conscience, our husband's desires (if we have one), and the wisdom of family and friends. We may have seasons when we need to pull back from work and others when we need to press in. Either way, we can trust in the sovereignty of God. He feeds the sparrow, causes the oak to grow, and raises the white lilies from their beds each spring. He knows our needs and will meet us where we are.

It was my sister-in-law who saw my daughter's first steps. They have a sweet, special relationship, so it felt appropriate. She caught them on video.

Lie: Guilt is just a part of being a working mom; you have to learn to live with it. If I were to gamble on one universal feeling that all moms have, I'd answer with two: joy and guilt. Joy, of course, because how could we not? And guilt—it may display as fear, anxiety, or uncertainty, but we all want to know, "Am I doing a good job?" And the voice usually whispers back, "Probably not."

While many talk about mom-guilt as a constant companion, what they don't often mention is that there are two kinds: true guilt and false guilt. True guilt is a result of sin. False guilt is the result of holding ourselves to standards we're not required to keep. I know well the temptations of the latter—like genuinely forgetting to sign the school paper or not seeing the scraped knee coming because I was with another child. These are the realities of being an embodied human, limited and bound to reality and biology.

But there is also a true, deserved guilt, and we all equally carry it: "Whoever keeps the whole law but fails in one point has become guilty of all of it"

(James 2:10). Every one of us has broken God's law, and we should feel right-ful guilt for our sin. Impatience for slow toddler feet, anger at spilled flour, gossip over the neighbor's fence.

Yet Christ came for both types of guilt. Not only to redeem our wrong thinking when we're carrying misplaced guilt but also to pay for our sins on the cross, giving us new life and righteousness in him. As moms—as peo-ple—we don't have to live with guilt as a constant shadow, whispering in our ear. In Christ, we have "good mom status" for eternity. As we trust him and seek him, we'll find freedom.

The Honest Truth

From time to time, I still get motivated to put "be available" on my to-do list. These days, it's less rigid and restricted, but it's still a reminder of the kind of mom I want to be as I walk this tension of work and motherhood. It helps me to be available not just for my kids but for my Lord. It prompts me to look around and be honest with the truth of my life in all my endeav-ors: Yes, I love my children. Yes, I love my work. Yes, it can be both. No, I cannot be everywhere at once. No, I will not get it all right. No, I don't have to carry guilt for that. No, that wasn't enough time. Yes, we should reevalu-ate. Yes, God sees me. Yes, God cares for me. Yes, Christ came for that. Yes, Christ paid for this. Yes, Christ is my all.

WHEN "REMEMBER THE GOSPEL" FEELS VAGUE

EMILY

Most married couples with children know daily life and shared responsibilities can fog our view of each other. Late night conversations and desserts at a local cafe become yawns, as you try to stay awake long enough to watch a short show together. You become experts in throwing dirty diapers like baseballs to each other so you can reach the trash can. Coffee chats include more things like "So did you ever find the pacifier under the crib last night?" and less "Tell me more about how you're feeling, dear." That's not to say that married couples with young kids aren't deeply committed and even passionately intimate, but the "first love" feeling can be hard to remember.

One year, around our anniversary, my husband and I stayed in and looked at old pictures and scrapbooks. We flipped the pages slowly, reminiscing about our favorite dates, the way we pursued each other, and the things we were first attracted to. We laughed about the "Remember when..." stories, flirting like young twenty-somethings along the way. By the end of the evening, it felt like someone wiped the fog from our glasses so we could see each other clearly again, realizing that not only did our love remain, but it was forged stronger by years of hard things and shared purpose.

God's Pattern for "Remembering" in the Bible

Especially when it comes to love, remembering is about not just drumming up memories but having a matured awareness of the way people and experiences have impacted our lives. We remember things all the time (for good and bad reasons), and we know how a memory can change our perspective on a current mood or situation. God created us this way, and he draws on our ability to remember in his Word by giving symbols, benchmarks, and stories that bring his goodness and faithfulness back to the forefront of the minds of his people, which in turn helps us ultimately *remember the gospel*.

When Noah and his family survived the flood, God put a rainbow in the sky so that every time people saw it, they would remember his rescue and promise. When Israel was delivered from Egypt, God had them observe festivals and traditions that reminded them of the Passover and of his provision in the desert. When he gave them the law and the ten commandments, he also wanted them to recite it each year so they could remember how to live. God wanted parents to pass along the epic narrative of their deliverance to each generation so that they would know Yahweh is God alone. Many of

David's psalms are about lamenting to God while remembering his promises, and many of the prophets reminded the people of Israel of God's love and commands, hoping they would repent.

This pattern is played out in the New Testament church as well, as the Gospels were recorded to remember who Jesus was and what he did in his time on Earth. And many of the letters to the early church focused first on explaining and remembering the work of Christ, drawing that to mind so that it would impact their lives and love for others. We're even given an account of the future restoration of God's people in Revelation, so we can remember what God is going to do in the future. The concept of remembering is crucial to our lives as believers.

Stop, Rest, and Remember

But even though we know the gospel is important, the cares of life fog our lenses. Our once clean glasses—seeing ourselves, our relationships, and our experiences in the context of God's saving work—become covered with the gook of social media distractions, conflicts with family members, diapers that need changing, work deadlines that are looming, health issues, and the demand to get dinner on the table ten minutes ago. Pretty soon, we're walking around looking at the world through the lens of our troubles, experiences, and culturally driven desires. We're stumbling along the path, we're tripping and falling over, we forget where we're even supposed to be going. Just like the daily doldrums of married life can cause us to forget the spark of love we share in covenant want with our spouses, the hardships of life can drown out the beauty of the gospel.

This is why we must stop and intentionally "remember the gospel." We must sit by the side of the road, take off our dirty glasses, and clean them.

Take time to read God's Word, the account of all he's already done and all he has yet to do.

Take time to pray and share our concerns, thinking about them in light of God's faithfulness.

Take time to read good books that point us to the gospel as others recount the goodness of God through Christ.

Take time to meet with other believers where we can sing God's praises and encourage one another to hold fast to the truth.

It's only after this type of stopping, resting, and remembering that we can stand back up with a renewed awareness of God's love for us, our love for him, and the unbreakable covenant he's made through the sacrifice of Christ. We can smile as we go forward, seeing life clearly again—all the good and perfect gifts that are from above, the way God has caused the lines to fall in good places for us (even if it's hard to understand at the moment).

When you're frustrated because you're knee-deep in Legos, wondering when you're going to get those overdue library books returned—*remember the gospel*: God cares for your heart and will help you persevere in the most mundane aspects of life when you turn to him.

When you're exhausted from another long night—*remember the gospel*: God gives you ultimate rest in Christ and can provide for your deepest needs, and you don't need to prove yourself. You can take a nap.

When you're bummed about skipping your Bible study—*remember the gospel*: Your sin is so deep that you couldn't rescue yourself; he had to rescue you through Jesus. Turn back to him, remember that first love, and rejoice at the fact that he'll keep you forever.

WHEN YOU THINK IT'S TOO HARD TO SERVE OUTSIDE YOUR HOME

LAURA

In these little years, it can be easy to convince myself it's not practical to serve outside my home. I have three under five who have only one (incredibly loud) vocal setting, and their favorite hobby is running in circles while holding breakable items.

But the truth is, I can't serve inside my home without serving outside my home. What I mean is, a vital part of raising my children to know and love the Lord is showing them that loving God means loving others. So while you likely won't find us at a soup kitchen in this season, you will find us doing seemingly small things in the home that matter outside of it.

Right now, one way that looks is making meals for new moms, the sick, or the elderly. Sometimes, it's for complete strangers. We head to the store to pick up ingredients, talking about how "these are not for us; they're for someone in need." It takes forever to make the meal, and there's lots of taste testing and a massive mess at the end. I literally plan an *entire* morning for it. We talk about how we're not going to eat the cookies we baked or the cider we bought, or the sausage in the lasagna—someone in need is. We talk about being Jesus's hands and feet and how the gospel is played out in the everyday making of meals and care packages.

While it sounds trivial, it's a hard lesson for small children. We drive to the house and drop it off, stopping to talk for a few minutes, the kids wondering why we don't go inside or play with toys. We get back in the car and talk about how people sometimes go through hard things and how bringing a meal is a way of loving them through it. We talk about wanting to be generous with our time, money, and talents. That we should use the things God has blessed us with to bless others.

It's simple stuff, but I pray it will make a profound impact on their future.

These little years are not "lost ministry" years; they're a chance to get creative with how we serve as mothers, knowing this time is a training ground for our children, a launchpad for them to begin to understand what a lifetime of godly service and ministry looks like in the everyday.

Because to serve the inside, you have to serve the outside too.

FOR WHEN
YOU ARE SAD

Nearly all moms know grief and its sting.
We detest sin and tremble at the horrors of it.
We feel sorrow and long for Christ to return and
for everything to be made new. Yet we are only
seeing one part of the story that God is writing.
It's often not until years later—or maybe not even
in our lifetime—that we will see and know all of
what God was doing for our good and his glory.

EMILY

WHEN YOU NEED HOPE

EMILY

"Everything is going to be okay."

This was the message our pastor comforted us with. And before he said it, he warned us that it might sound trite...but instead of falling on calloused ears, I'm pretty sure most of the congregation were holding back tears of deep comfort. As I thought about it later, it's something we often lose sight of in the weary days of motherhood as well.

Everything is going to be okay if you are in Christ.

Not necessarily because God is going to change your circumstances.

Not because you're going to suddenly start feeling less tired.

Not because your husband is going to start helping with more things.

Not because your kids are going to obey immediately or be perfectly behaved.

Not because the situation that's been bothering you for months is going to finally be resolved.

But everything is going to be eventually and eternally okay because Jesus rose from the dead and conquered sin. He is coming again to restore all things to himself. He is going to give believers a new body that will never die, and we will live free from sin and full of joy in our Creator forever and ever.

We will sing the new song with all the saints, and it will be said of us, "'Blessed are the dead who die in the Lord from now on.' 'Blessed indeed,' says the Spirit, 'that they may rest from their labors, for their deeds follow them!'" (Revelation 14:13).

We can be Christian moms who *rest* because we have the ultimate hope. Sing your new song now, and if you can't have joy in today's circumstances, have joy in Christ and what's to come.

WHEN LIFE DOESN'T GO TO PLAN

LAURA

The shouts of the world tell us mothers, "You only live once, so you must live it to the fullest. Don't die never having started that business, written that book, or pursued that dream."

"You deserve it," they say. "You'll regret it if you don't," they tell us.

But is that really true? That we only have one life to live, and we must do it all now?

For those of us in Christ, we live twice.

We don't have to "do it all" here because we'll do even better things on the shores of glory. We don't have to achieve every dream, travel the globe, or experience every thrill, because whatever joy it is we think we'll find, it will pale in comparison to what awaits in our second life.

It's good practice for us to pause and ask the question, "What is my purpose here? What will make a meaningful life?" Is it, as they say, the pursuit of our own dreams? If that's the case, I wonder if all of us will feel unfulfilled and purposeless because reality tends to barrel through dreams like a hurricane. It's not that dreams are bad; it's just that none of us *have a right to a certain life.*

If we're asking what our purpose is, it's for glory. But not our own. God's. If you are mourning the path your life has taken, perhaps this will encourage you: In Christ, this life is not all there is.

Of course, in his kindness, some dreams will be fulfilled here. But for all the others, remember: Save your dreams for your second life. For there they will be different, better, and more wonderful than you ever could have imagined in your first.

WHEN YOU DON'T FEEL BLESSED

EMILY

We tend to think a blessed motherhood is one full of good experiences—with little noise and few tears. One with combed hair, matching outfits, and trips to museums or boutique donut shops. As we press deeper, perhaps we define *blessing* as carrying a child in our womb, in our arms, or on our hips. We affirm that blessing means hearing laughter, tending to owies, and instructing children in the ways of eternal life.

All of these things are true—blessing takes many forms. Moms have many obvious reasons to give thanks.

But God also showers his blessing through clouds and rain, through a season of diagnosis or while we wait for a child's heart to soften. He blesses us as we accept the sorrows of motherhood through the lens of his character and his Word.

And blessing most surely and eternally comes as we confess our sin and need for a Savior, resting fully in Christ's righteousness. We are blessed because through him, we have a way to the Father—a voice in prayer, a covering of righteousness, a promise of his presence. We are blessed because filled with the Spirit, we can follow his counsel and trust his ways.

In our many experiences of motherhood, in our ups and downs, in our happy and hard moments, we're ultimately blessed because of the One who became a curse for us. We rejoice because Christ made a way for us to be with God forever.

If your faith is in him, then no matter what you face today with the children in your care, you are a mother who is blessed.

WHEN GRIEF LINGERS

LAURA

Some things cannot be resolved; they can only be carried in your hands. For a time, these things live in your interlaced fingers. But slowly, the thing will move to your back—a burden at first, then a shadow. But it's always there, taking on life in one form or another. Sometimes heavy and painful, other times, simply like a light touch on your skin.

Miscarriage, disability, death, illness, violence against the innocent—the worst of the curse hangs like a noose over the earth. When these things affect you personally, it can feel like you have been abandoned by God. You wonder why he is distant and why he seems to have forgotten you.

So what do you do when how you feel doesn't match your theology? Is it okay to be honest about how you feel? Are you a fraud because you know better than to think God has left you? Is it wrong to ask God to explain himself?

Over the years, I've learned that the tension of how one feels versus what one knows is the frequent companion of the Christian. We can and should tell God how we feel; he already knows anyway. But it's all about how we approach the throne. The temptation is to approach God in anger, arrogantly asking him to give a tell-all. But God opposes the proud (James 4:6).

Instead, God asks us for a "broken and contrite heart" (Psalm 51:17). When we cry out like the psalmists—in honest anguish for God to help us understand his ways so we can draw near to him—God hears, God binds, and God loves.

In humility, you can ask God why. To ask him to be true to who you know he is. To ask him to strengthen your heart, do justice, have mercy, and incline his ear to your distress.

When I do this, I'll be honest, I typically don't receive the answer I started out looking for. But I do find my heart comforted, my theology deepened, and my feelings realigned to the truth. These things don't remove the suffering, but they give me the endurance to carry the hard. The shadow is still there, always a companion, but being real with God reminds me that he is greater than my suffering. And sometimes, with enough time, I do get the answers I sought.

Friend, don't be afraid to speak aloud things that feel like they shouldn't be said. Be vulnerable with God. You can come to him at any time, with anything. He has not forgotten you. He loves you and cares for you. You only have to ask him to remind you.

WHEN YOU FEEL
LIKE A NOBODY

LAURA

If you have come to the end of your day feeling like the outcast, the failure, the one that never gets it right—if you feel like a blunder of a mother, remember:

He is greater than your fears, impatience, and anger.

He is greater than your mistakes, flaws, and self-hate.

He is greater than your timidity, pride, and failures.

He is greater than all of it.

There is no condemnation in Christ. In him you are holy, righteous, redeemed, and beautiful. Whatever you did today is forgiven and erased because of his work on the cross.

Trust the One that makes all things new, each and every day.

Shake off the guilt, live in freedom.

You may feel like a nothing nobody, but in him, in his greatness, you shine like the sun in the glory of Christ.

Worship and walk confidently in this truth.

WHEN YOU DON'T GET
WHAT YOU WANT

LAURA

There are many incredible things about being a Christian, but perhaps one of the most stunning things is the hope of heaven. While there are many applications to knowing that someday we'll live forever in heaven with Christ, one of my personal favorites is an understanding that we don't have to get everything we want in this life. Because someday, every need, every want, every desire we have will be fulfilled when we reach eternity's shores.

This changes everything for you, Mom. An eternal perspective can change how you order your time, who you spend your days with, how you talk, and what you do. When the promise of heaven becomes your orbit, you can say, "I want to give it all for Christ now because I know that I've got eternity and the glory that awaits me there."

You don't have to spend your days fearfully hoarding your resources, saving storehouses with angst for a rainy day, or selfishly protecting what you have, because Christian love is generous and rooted in trust in God. You're to be overflowing with generosity, abounding in love, and filled to the max with the fruit of the Spirit. Like Paul, you can be "poured out as a drink offering" (Philippians 2:17) because you aren't seeking your reward here and now. You're looking ahead to heaven, knowing true happiness, true joy—everything you've ever wanted—you'll get someday in eternity.

WHEN THE FALL ISN'T FUNNY

EMILY

There's something powerful about a protagonist's smile. Usually around the climax or falling action of a great redemptive story, there comes a point when the main character or hero doles a mortal blow to the villain—but the villain doesn't know it yet. The villain still approaches with their sinister speech, laughing maniacally and thinking they've won, but the hero knows something he doesn't—and he cracks a smile. Suddenly, the villain loses his footing and falls off a cliff or sees all of his plans laid to waste and reversed into the hero's favor. The villain laughed, but the protagonist got the last one.

When it comes to our fears and our foes, it's hard to imagine ourselves laughing. There is a sober and serious nature to the fear of losing personal or religious freedoms, a predictable paycheck, or our health as we care for our children. After all, our personal struggle with sin and suffering in life is a terrible reality—the Fall isn't funny.

But what if we knew that in an ultimate way, our fears weren't that frightening? What if the snake had no fangs, the dragon was about to meet his destruction, and the enemy's loss was sure? What if we believe that because of Christ, death has no sting and actually means more life? Could we crack a smile? Might we even be able to laugh in the face of hard and terrifying things?

If we are moms who have faith in the ultimate hero, Jesus Christ, and we believe in his ultimate victory, then laughter can become part of our repertoire. We can stare with soberness but also crack a smile. We can laugh through tears, smile at the end of a lament, and have light hearts in dark times.

Our laughter is a witness to the world that Christ gets the last laugh. Our ability to bring appropriate levity to fearful times means there is greater hope. We don't want to crush hurting people with an ill-timed joke, and there are often long seasons for tears before we're ready to remember they will be wiped away. But as someone reminded me recently—don't just look at the dark narrative (the painful results of the Fall) but also resolve to see the redemptive one (the many gifts of God in a given situation). As we recount even his smallest act of faithfulness, we can bask in the light. And in some cases, laughing at the future is also a great way to remind ourselves and others that our Rescuer will soon declare victory.

The villain might be laughing, but he's about to meet his end. Take heart and crack a smile.

BECAUSE "BEST OF" MOMENTS AREN'T ONLY HAPPY THINGS

EMILY

Have you ever thought about your "best of" moments in motherhood? I easily remember the hospital rooms where I labored and gave birth to each of our five children—holding them on my chest for the first time or visiting them in the NICU. I also think of the day our son with developmental delays used a walker independently for the first time or when our children were each dedicated at church.

While these "best of" moments are big, I think of others that are small. For instance, I have a favorite memory with my oldest son when he was just a toddler. I sat at a park table and watched him eat crackers as the sun shone on our faces during an unusually warm day in March. Nothing epic happened, but the moment still makes my highlight reel.

The thing I observe about my "best of" moments is that they are high-contrast moments in motherhood—the ones where love and beauty and goodness prevailed even in the midst of something hard.

When I think about the highlight reel of the life of Christ, a similar theme rings true. The Gospels (Matthew, Mark, Luke, and John) are sort of their own collection of "best of" moments, because John notes that Jesus's life and works couldn't be contained in all the books in the world (John 21:25). We might think that the Son of God's best moments wouldn't include suffering, but his highlight reel includes more pain than ours—and more glory. In the desert, his perfect obedience glorified God in the face of Satan's hostile temptations. Before the Sanhedrin, his spotless record put whitewashed tombs to shame as he suffered an unjust trial. At the cross, Jesus took our sin and shame while the Father turned his face away. Outside of the empty tomb, his beating heart was miraculous after the sting of death.

In light of God's big redemption story, it's no wonder that our "best of" moments aren't only happy things. The joy felt in the morning is ever so wonderful because of the refreshment it provides after a night of weeping.

BECAUSE YOU WERE NOT
MEANT TO MOM ALONE

LAURA

Neither of us felt equipped to be meeting together. Me because it was embarrassing just how much help I needed. And she because she didn't think she had any help to offer. She had twenty years on me, and when I saw her, I thought, "I want to be like her when I grow up." So with a deep breath and a leap of faith, I asked her to disciple me.

We met in the margins, maybe once a month. Over and over again, she repeated the gospel to me. We were both imperfect, both needy, both ill-equipped. But I soaked up her wisdom like a dry sponge, and she told me it went both ways—much to my disbelief. We were better together.

We are not meant to mom alone. No matter how much help the internet can be, no online community can offer a hug, hand you a tissue, watch

your children, or bring you a meal in a pinch. The women God has placed near you may not remember how to drop the evening nap or be as passionate about a certain school choice as you are, but if they love God as you do, they can remind you of the gospel—a far more important bond than anything else in motherhood.

If we all band together, one mom helping another, none of us will be alone in this journey. So, let's lock arms, learning and growing from one another, being brave to trust God to provide where we lack. God is bigger than our imperfections and insecurities, and he uses them to draw us and others to himself.

We can't do this motherhood journey alone, and God hasn't asked us to.

WHEN YOU FEEL DISCONTENT

_____

EMILY

Do you ever find yourself longing for the next thing?

In the baby years, I looked forward to the day when everyone would put on their own shoes or buckle themselves into the car. In the heat of summer, I start to imagine afternoons at the apple orchard or the cozy warmth of a fire. Every few months, it seems like these thoughts catch me off guard. Just a few weeks ago, I couldn't wait for summer break, afternoons at the swimming pool, and evenings in the backyard, and now I'm sighing about late nights and lack of routine as I look forward to the rhythms of the school year.

In these moments, when I find myself squirming in my seat, wanting a time of year or stage of parenting to be over because it's getting old, I have to counsel my heart with truth.

I was made to long for what's coming. I'm not fully at home in this world, and deep down, I know there is something fuller and better coming because I trust in Christ. As my heart looks forward to better things, I can place that longing even further into the future where it belongs—in the consummation of God's redemptive story.

I can ask for strength to be content in today's circumstances. This comes through Christ when I believe that he has purposes for me today—even if today has hard or undesirable things. This is the moment for my faithfulness, and I need the Spirit's help.

I can be sure that in tomorrow's stage or season, there will be fresh challenges and sorrows that I don't know about yet. My hope is not in the next thing or the lifting of this trial or monotony—it's in Christ.

It's normal and even good that we have excitement for the next thing in motherhood, but let's not miss the work that God is doing today or neglect faithfulness as we look forward to what's ahead. Let's be moms who long for the greatest "later" with Christ as we rest in what he has for us today.

WHEN YOU'VE LOST
WHO YOU ARE

LAURA

One night, I confessed to my small group that ever since my daughter was diagnosed with disabilities, I'd been struggling to come to terms with my new identity as a "mom to a child with a disability." I felt like I had all these new responsibilities, a new day-to-day, and a new future. I told them I didn't really know who I was anymore.

And then my friend, softly, sweetly, ever-so-kindly spoke up, "But if your identity is in Christ, who you are doesn't really change, does it?"

Maybe for you, it's not a new diagnosis for your child; maybe you're the "working mom," the "adoptive mom," the "single mom," the "twin mom," the "homeschool mom," the "miscarriage mom," the "part-time mom," the "mom who can't get her act together." I don't know what it is that's flipping your world upside down, but what I can tell you is these things that are consuming your time, thoughts, and cares right now are not who you are.

If you're in Christ, you are his. Your identity is in him. That means no matter how life plays out, you can rest secure in the grace that has been given to you—a grace that meets every new trial, temptation, and tornado of life.

When God calls you to a difficult path, he does not leave you alone, scraping by in isolation. He equips you, provides for you, and tenderly cares for you all the way through it.

Though we can act like it sometimes, we don't subsist on our own merits, talents, or skills. Thank goodness! We abide in Christ, which means we subsist on all that *he has*. We have Jesus's endless well of patience, joy, peace, diligence, long-suffering, and self-control as we go about our days. And best of all, we share in the royal inheritance.

When we can't see the light anymore, we can remember: We have a hope that will last far beyond this life.

So you can lay down those feelings of "I don't know who I am," because if you are in Christ, who you are hasn't changed. It doesn't matter what you have or haven't done or what has or hasn't happened to you—you are made in God's image and cherished by him. Who you are is his precious daughter, inherently loved, valued, and declared worthy by him.

FOR WHEN YOU NEED STRENGTH TO KEEP GOING

───────

Jesus Christ is the only perfect person who ever lived, and he is a firm foundation. He's never changing. He should be the biggest one in our lives and in our hearts and the one who we place all our weight and expectation on. Everybody else is human—think accordingly.

EMILY

WHEN YOU'RE WONDERING WHAT GOD HAS CALLED YOUR FAMILY TO

EMILY

If you're anything like me, you've wondered, "How do I know what God has called our family to do in his name?" While the answer to that question is personal, prayerful, and best sought in community, here are a few guidepost questions that have helped me.

What things has God already clearly called us to do in Scripture? For instance, it's already clear that he loves children, widows, orphans, the lost, the sick, the sojourner, the poor, and so on—and we know we are supposed to love others in the name of Jesus, be part of a local church body, do things from faith with the fruit of the Spirit, and spread the gospel with those we interact with. How are we doing or pursuing those things in the life and place that God gave us?

What relationships or circumstances has God already placed in your care? Are you married? Do you have kids? Do you have extended family that need love/help/support? Are you part of a church family? Are you in a job where you have hurting/lost co-workers? Who do you interact with regularly? Do you have neighbors or friends who don't know Jesus? These are your people!

What is your heart attitude and goal in the "everyday" moments? Are you always hoping for a more radical opportunity to come along so you can prove your love and service for God, or do you consider the small, mundane moments opportunities for acts of obedience and worship? Are you considering how to use the everyday opportunities for ministry? What would it look like if you viewed these daily interactions as chances to share the gospel with others?

What things are you passionate about or particularly good at doing? Is there something your husband loves being involved in or has a heart for? Is there a particular ministry or way of life—consistent with the call of the Great Commission—that you can't get off your hearts? Is there something people acknowledge that you as a family do really well just naturally? This might be a unique area where God is calling you to ministry.

Prayerfully considering these questions with your spouse is a great way to start the conversation about what God has called you to do. In some seasons, it might mean more radical-looking sacrifices, and in other seasons, it might mean being faithful in the ordinary work and family life that God has already given you. And remember—you may never know in this life how God uses your family to spread the gospel and impact the kingdom!

WHEN YOU FEEL LIKE
YOUR WORK IS SMALL

EMILY

Do you ever feel like your work is just too small? Loving your family as you clean throw-up off couch cushions, make chicken tenders in the air fryer, and actually get the laundry folded *and* put away feels monumental sometimes. But does it really matter in the grand scheme of things?

Sometimes it's hard for us to properly value our work in the kingdom of God.

In Numbers 3–4, there was another group of people who were given various jobs to serve the Lord in building and transporting the tabernacle. They each had unique burdens to carry—from the amazing and grand curtains and the Ark of the Covenant to the pegs, cords, equipment, and accessories. How would it feel to be the person who carried the pegs when your friend got to help carry the Ark?

But carrying the pegs was still valuable work. Each piece of the tabernacle and its care was important. And this job was specifically called out by

God in the Scriptures and given by God to particular people. It was holy work.

Today, we're not literally carrying pegs for God, but most moms understand work that feels small. And in a world that says we can always achieve our dreams and manifest our destiny or that we deserve to have the life we always wanted, it can be even harder to joyfully accept the work the Lord has given us to do, no matter the immediate visible impact.

As we think of the man in Numbers carrying pegs, let's also remember the greater work he was a part of—the right worship of God's covenant people as they followed God's commands. And today, we do our work not only for the Lord but for his greater purposes alongside his people. Each believer has a valuable role to play! We can work heartily, being obedient and faithful—not because of how impressive our job is but because we serve the Lord our God.

The small work is still holy work, if done for him.

BECAUSE THE GREAT COMMISSION IS FOR YOU TOO

EMILY

The Great Commission isn't just for missionaries; it's for moms too. Our children need the gospel. Our children need to be taught to observe Jesus's commands. Our children need to know that Jesus is with them.

So while you might not be able to go across the ocean to make disciples, you can make disciples at the breakfast table, or before bedtime, or while you're driving around town. Teach them to observe all that he has commanded, knowing that Jesus is with you too.

"Go, therefore, and make disciples of all nations, baptizing them in the name of the Father and of the Son and of the Holy Spirit, teaching them to observe everything I have commanded you. And remember, I am with you always, to the end of the age" (Matthew 28:19-20 CSB).

WHEN YOUR CHILDREN ARE NOT "GOOD"

LAURA

Often I find myself looking for my worth in my children. Not consciously, of course, but I monitor their behavior, responses, and actions and from there make a judgment call on myself.

I am good if they were good.

I am bad if they were not good.

I find my satisfaction in a low number of tantrums, a constant flow of p's and q's, and how pious and obedient they were to my requests.

But what God is teaching me—not just little by little but in big, scary, in-my-face ways—is that I cannot expect my children to be my source of life.

To expect our children to be our hope, our joy, our reward, is a burden unfairly placed. Our true source of life, satisfaction, love, peace, and worth can only be found in one place: the redeeming work of Christ on the cross.

This is good news, Mom! Because this frees both you and your children from a struggle you cannot win. You stop placing unfair expectations on your children to be what they cannot be, and they are lifted from the burden of striving to be what they will never be.

We already have all we need in our Savior, so let's look to him to be our source of life. He is the only one who can declare us good, and because of Christ, he already has. In him, no matter what kind of day you or your kids are having—good or bad—you are loved, cared for, and made holy. This is good news.

WHEN THE KIDS WANT
TO BE JUST LIKE YOU

_____

EMILY

"Mom, are you doing Bible study now? Can I come? I want to get my Bible study out!"

Little pajama feet pitter-patter up the stairs into the kitchen to grab their container full of nearly dried-out markers and well-used notebooks. They find their small Bibles and negotiate whose name is on the front, double-checking by investigating the types of stickers they find inside the cover ("Oh, Thomas the train—that's mine!!"). They spread their materials out beside me, climbing onto stools at the kitchen island.

Honestly, *I groan a little bit.* I've been quietly working on my own study for only ten minutes when I'm caught, and everyone feels the need to join me. But deep down, my heart is glad that these hearts are soft to the Word of God and feel compelled to sit down next to me, at least pretending to read it.

With all of them being under five, very little structured activity actually happens. Instead, they grab markers from one another, get caught coloring directly on the counter, drop their notebooks on the floor, and just generally interrupt mommy's "quiet" time of the morning.

My oldest leans over and asks, "Why do you get to write in your Bible? What are you marking?" And despite my temptation to push him off—because I actually *do* want to get through the passage—I explain my method the best I can. He asks me to read the chapter, which he listens to a few sentences of before starting a drawing of himself riding in a boat with Grandma.

I sigh and wonder, "Is all of this even worth it?" just as the toddler in the high chair noisily smacks the counter, screaming for his own marker.

But deep down, I know God is faithful and his Word does not return void. I remember that Jesus made disciples by walking with people in their everyday lives, engaging with the noise, the mess, and the brokenness. He modeled a love for God and a commitment to his Father's Word in all kinds of circumstances. And a little part of letting Jesus reign in our house is displaying the same type of love in front of my own children. If my "love for God" is actually just a pious act—someday they will see right through me.

If you're feeling discouraged—worried that you aren't doing enough to form your children spiritually—start by focusing on your own relationship with God for a while. Sit down and consistently study his Word. Practice prayer and repentance when God prompts you to confess and walk according to your new life. When you live this way, it will spill all over the whole house…just like their sippy cups (*am I right?!*).

From there—by God's grace—pray your kids will follow. Pray that they will be drawn to the amazing, transforming power of the gospel and the living Word that you love so much. And when that happens, don't get frustrated if they ask to join your "quiet" time. Rejoice at the good work God is doing in them and through you.

BECAUSE THE BEST GIFTS CAN'T BE PURCHASED WITH MONEY

LAURA

As parents, it's easy to focus on investing in material things and experiences for our children so that we forget what will truly give them lasting success and happiness in this life—and forevermore.

Yet our greatest good (and our children's)—the thing that makes us the most "successful," joyful, and happy people—is something that can't be purchased with money.

Yet our Father God spared no expense.

God paid the highest price for our lives in the punishment of his own innocent Son. Where we often use our resources for our own gain and our own glory, he sacrificed his own Son for our gain and *his* glory. He understands our needs go beyond the physical to a need of the heart. Instead of focusing on giving us "stuff," he gives us what we really need: himself.

When we recognize the price paid for our relationship with God, it puts everything into perspective. Remember what will last: God, his Word, and his people. Invest in those more than in earthly things money can buy.

WHEN YOU LOVE
JESUS MORE

EMILY

As I tuck my oldest son into bed, we talk quietly, exploring different worlds through imaginative stories. I tell him about rescue workers, brave puppy dogs, and even royal princes who travel long distances to defeat evil. Sometimes, our stories veer off the genre of fairy tale into the territory of truth regarding heaven and the new earth. This, I tell my son, is the *ultimate* rescue story.

My son leans over and asks, "Will you and Daddy be there in heaven?" expressing his desire to be with us forever. I calm his heart, letting him know that yes, we will be there. But I don't move on before telling him there is someone more important for him to be with, and that person is Jesus. I explain as plainly as I can to a preschooler that the best thing about heaven won't be the lack of tears, the healed boo-boos, the fellowship with family, or the joyful songs. The most wonderful thing about heaven will be seeing, knowing, and treasuring Jesus face-to-face, worshipping him and glorifying God forever. Jesus is the ultimate treasure. He is also the ultimate rescuer and the person who Mommy loves more than anything else.

What I speak to my son in the dimly lit bedtime hour is the truth. With the Spirit in me, I can say with all joy and seriousness that Jesus is my greatest love. But my present life in the flesh means I don't always act that way. Even in my best attempts, I fail greatly and find myself worshipping other loves. I enjoy the approval of my children and my friends, I lay down too much for the sake of worldly achievements, I pursue satisfaction in entertainment and social media, and I desire for all those under my reign to make me look good. To my child, it might even seem offensive to hear I love someone else more, but ultimately, it's the greatest gift I can give.

If my son could understand, I would tell him this is such a good gift because…

When Mommy loves Jesus more than her own peace and quiet, she can graciously endure the loud whines of tired children, putting their need for firm, compassionate training above her desires for them to leave her alone.

When Mommy loves Jesus more than her dreams and achievements, she can invest deeply in the discipleship of her children, trusting God with the limitations he brings in each season.

When Mommy loves Jesus more than approval, she can seek long-term good for the souls of her children instead of gaining the short-term relief that comes from satisfying their cravings.

When Mommy loves Jesus more than her own domestic kingdom, she can discipline with calm justice, knowing that her and her children's offenses are equally egregious and equally atoned for.

When Mommy loves Jesus more than the title of "Mom," she can entrust the souls of her children to their faithful Creator while continuing to serve mightily for their good.

When Mommy loves Jesus more than her children's good behavior, she can patiently exposit the loveliness of the gospel over many months and years, instead of finding temporal satisfaction in immediate external changes.

When Mommy loves Jesus more than her personal rights, she can sweep crumbs off the floor for the thousandth time without grumbling or complaining because she remembers her Savior, who humbled himself to the lowest position.

When Mommy loves Jesus more than her comfort, she can get out of bed repeatedly; sacrificing years of sleep to nurture, support, pray for, and minister to her children.

When Mommy loves Jesus more than her entertainment, she can use her precious personal moments to invest in the eternal knowledge of God's Word instead of automatically binge-watching her favorite show.

When Mommy loves Jesus more than her social media following, she can appropriately protect and celebrate the lives of her husband and children instead of exploiting them for her personal gain.

When Mommy loves Jesus more than her ability to control her circumstances, she can trust God, not fearing anything that is frightening in this world because she knows the God who overcame the grave.

While the reality of these things might be exceedingly difficult to obtain, and the applications will look different for every mom, the importance of making Jesus our greatest love cannot be overstated. When we fail to do this and instead make good things too important, our children are shortchanged. They might get the gift of good nutrition, wise direction, athletic training, popularity, or material wealth from us, but they don't get the eternal gift of the gospel.

And for every mommy out there who read those truths and grieved the state of her own heart, there is still an opportunity to glorify God. Because you can still show Jesus's greatness as you repent and remind your children that you are not their ultimate hope. "Mommy" will fail, so they must rest their hearts on someone eternally satisfying.

So, as awkward and abrasive as it might sound to my son's little ears, I will continue to tell him (and all my children, for that matter) that I love Jesus more. I pray that someday, my son will be able to tell his children the same truth amid fairy tales, rescue stories, and dimly lit bedtime snuggles.

WHEN YOU CAN'T SEE GOD'S HELP

EMILY

In motherhood, it's easy to see all the things we lack—all the ways we fall short. We heave a heavy sigh and wonder if we'll ever get it right. Hope for ourselves and our children slips from our grasp faster than a bag of fruit snacks after a morning at the park.

So we pray and we ask God for help. We think about how much he loves us and is for us. We remember how strong and powerful, present and capable he is. But...then what? We still *feel* just as weak as we did thirty seconds ago. Has anything changed?

By faith, we can be confident that if we're in Christ, then his Spirit is strengthening us every step of the way. Our hearts might not instantly swell with assurance, and our steps might not immediately bound into a steady pace, but his strength is still there.

Strength in Christ can look like...

Moving forward in obedience to God, even though you're tired and you're not sure what the outcome will be.

Having hope in God and his promises, believing that even though things look bleak right now, he is caring for and providing for you.

Turning to the Lord over and over again instead of giving in or giving up and going your own way.

Having a peaceful heart, even when you're struggling or circumstances don't look the way you expected.

Continuing to love others, putting one hand and foot in front of the other out of a desire to serve the Lord and glorify him.

Oftentimes it's hard to see or feel the reality of this type of strength until you turn around and look behind you. When you see that mom from six months ago or two years ago who was struggling and feeling like she wasn't enough, you suddenly realize that God helped her persevere. God provided for her and did a mighty work in and through her, despite her lack. Then you'll breathe a sigh of praise.

Just as faith moves us forward without sight, sometimes it also moves us forward without feeling. But oh, his strength is absolutely there.

WHEN YOU NEED A FRIEND

LAURA

It's easy to dream up the perfect friend. Usually they dress like us, talk like us, and live like us. But the reality is no friend can be all things for us. Instead, it probably looks like one friend who is incredible at asking questions and getting you to open up, and another friend who always comes prepared and has "extra" when you're in need. (These friends are like the Swiss Army knives of moms!) Another friend will be your go-to when you're struggling with a child, and another will have the best clothing and makeup tips.

While some of us will find that BFF who feels like everything to us, most of us will have several friends who fill different needs. And no matter what, we all need a wide variety of friends. It's how God designed community.

As I've moved a few times to entirely new communities in motherhood, I've learned to lay down my expectations on friendships and be open to whomever God has for me. And what I've come to find is that surprising friendships are often the sweetest ones. A mom with kids older than mine helps me think through boundaries, a college student who babysits my kids teaches me about what the next generation values and cares about, a grandmother reminds me to pursue holiness, and a friend I initially thought I had absolutely nothing in common with over time became the person I laugh more with than anyone else.

These unexpected friendships are the ones that most often challenge me to think differently or view my situation in a unique light. They are the ones that drive me to be a better mother or wife in a new way—and most importantly, push me to pursue Jesus more.

So if you are starting fresh in a new town or are just feeling lonely for friendship, let me encourage you to let go of the mental picture of a perfect friend. Ask Christ to bring friends into your life, and ask him to make you open to them—no matter who they are. Pray that he will bring women into your life who challenge you to pursue him more and that you will be satisfied with whom he brings, even if they don't look like your expectations.

Let yourself be surprised by a friendship. We serve a big God; he knows more than you what your needs are, and he will provide.

WHEN YOU FORGET YOUR MISSION

EMILY

When it comes to being a family who wants to live for Christ, it's easy to use others as the measure of our own success. As we admire what God is doing through the lives of other families, we can be tempted to believe a narrative of condemnation about our own calling.

Without even realizing it, our mission can become about a Christian version of "keeping up with the Joneses," wanting to be approved of and impress those around us instead of resting in the full righteousness Jesus purchased on our behalf.

We can rest in his grace when we remember that every family is going to live out the Great Commission differently...

Some will adopt or foster orphans.

Some will have dinner with strangers.

Some will make meals for recovering friends.

Some will serve in formal ministry.

Some will homeschool.

Some will be very involved in the local school system.

Some will hold influence in the community.

Some will volunteer at clinics and nonprofits.

Some will travel or move to other countries.

Some will be faithful in their own home and family environment.

Some will do quiet things that will only be seen by God.

God hasn't called all Christian families to a specific mold, and he certainly isn't asking us to show off our deeds for the sake of our own glory. Instead, God has called us to keep our eyes and hearts fixed on Jesus, ready to obey his call for our lives, knowing that we live in service to him for his glory.

So today, if you feel like you are dragging the weight of condemnation and wondering whether you are doing enough, stop and pray. Ask God what he would have you do to love and serve those around you well, for his glory. Ask him how you can run the race set before you, so you can shed the fear of man and get going.

There is no perfect version of a "gospel-centered" family, but instead, there's a beautiful tapestry of gifts, passions, circumstances, and resources woven together in obedience to reach every culture and community with the good news of Jesus Christ.

BECAUSE FORMAL TEACHING IS IMPORTANT TOO

———————

LAURA

I claim I would do anything for God. I profess a faith that says I am willing to suffer for him—even to the point of death. But if I'm not careful, I tend to treat God like an old trinket, cast off in a corner, gathering dust, only coming out on Sunday mornings or when I suddenly have a need.

It's a simple question, really: "Do you love Jesus more than anything?"

And if the answer is "Yes," then wouldn't we want to bring God to the forefront, bubbling over with excitement and joy over what he has done for us? Wouldn't we tell our friends, family, and children about him?

While much of our faith is passed on to our children informally, as moms, we still need to sit down and teach our children the important truths of the Christian life. These times of family worship teach our children in a bright and obvious way that the gospel is everything to us. They train our children to be aware of their desperate need for a Savior—of their need for guidance, intervention, and reconciliation.

Intentional teaching brings out the "why" of the truths you naturally show to your children by your actions. It brings understanding to what you model throughout the week. It brings the picture of God and the Bible full circle in a child's view.

Formally passing on your faith says, "Mom loves God and the Bible. Mom learns and grows from the Bible. Mom talks to God. And Mom loves God so much that she wants you to know how to do this too."

In truth, family devotions are not just for our children; they are for our own edification as well. Because taking time to formally teach our children about biblical truths teaches us much: to be patient, to be thoughtful, to see the beauty in God's redemptive plan from the wonder of a child.

These are crucial years, Mom. Let's view intentional teaching as not a burden but a delight—a chance to display our love and devotion for the One who has done so much for us.

BECAUSE THE GOSPEL MATTERS

LAURA

You remember holding your baby close to your heart,
   feeding them solids for the very first time,
   and watching their chubby legs dance in the saucer.
   You remember wondering if you were giving them the right nutrition,
   the right bedtime routine,
   the right storybook Bible.
   You remember wondering, *Does the gospel matter in this season of motherhood?*
   And you found that it did.
   But babies grow. You've packed up the clothes, given away the stroller, and tossed out the pacifiers.
   Your kids have grown, and so have you.
   Now you have school decisions, evening activities, and "When do I get them a phone?"
   So you ask, *Does the gospel matter in this season of motherhood?*
   Oh, friend, it does.
   It met you in the days of up-all-night newborns, sweet-and-sticky toddlers.
   It will meet you in these bright and beautiful middle years.
   The gospel changes everything.
   In every season, at every stage, in every moment of motherhood, there is a risen motherhood available for all of us.

WHEN YOU DON'T FEEL LIKE YOUR EFFORTS MATTER

EMILY

In truth, it doesn't feel like our little efforts to share Christ with our children really add up. Reading the Bible here or there, praying inconsistently before meals, pointing out the beauty of God in everyday moments—these seem like small, feeble attempts at passing along our faith, but *each effort matters*.

Not because we are awesome or have lovely words, but because faith comes by hearing the Word of God and the gospel.

Because the Word of God is living and active.

Because the Word goes out and does the work—all we have to do is be faithful to carry the message.

No matter how weary you are today, remember to carry the message of grace to your children.

Carry it to the crib.

Carry it to the playground.

Carry it to the minivan.

Carry it to the dinner table.

Carry it to the bedside.

Carry it with confidence in God's ability to do big things with your small, everyday investments.

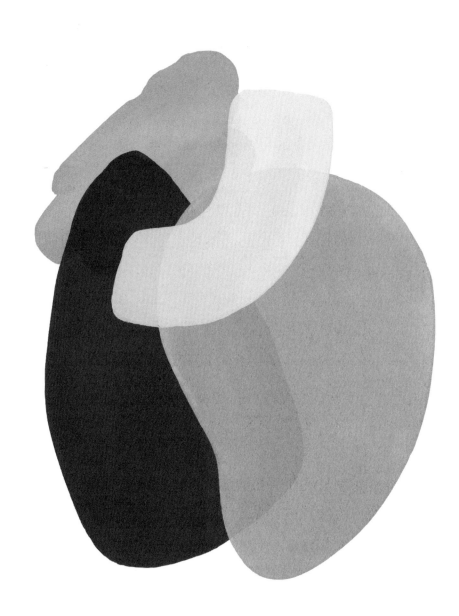

NOTES

72   Lyrics from Robert Lowry and Annie S. Hawks, "I Need Thee Every Hour, Most Gracious Lord" (1872), Hymnary.org, https://hymnary.org/text/i_need_thee_every_hour_most_gracious_lor.

112   A version of this article first appeared as "One Important Question for Social-Media Use," The Gospel Coalition, December 13, 2019, https://www.thegospelcoalition.org/article/one-important-question-social-media-use/. Included with permission from The Gospel Coalition.

149   A version of this article first appeared as "Sabbath Rest Is for Busy Moms, Too," The Gospel Coalition, February 10, 2019, https://www.thegospelcoalition.org/article/sabbath-rest-moms/. Included with permission from The Gospel Coalition.

225   A version of this article first appeared as "When Mommy Loves Jesus More," For the Church, May 31, 2016, https://ftc.co/resource-library/blog-entries/when-mommy-loves-jesus-more/. Included with permission from For the Gospel.

TWO MOMS—ONE MISSION

Emily A. Jensen (emilyajensen.com) and **Laura Wifler** (laurawifler.com) are the cofounders of Risen Motherhood. Through their ministry, podcast, and books, they help moms connect their faith to their motherhood. Sisters-in-law Emily and Laura live in central Iowa with their families.

Discover more from Emily and Laura to help you live out gospel motherhood, grow spiritually strong, and build your child's empathy and imagination.

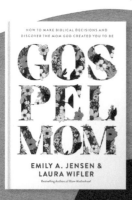

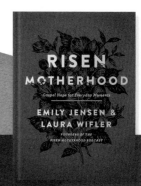

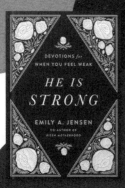
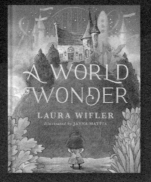

Available wherever books are sold.